150

For Robert,

My Brother in the Work
who has shared with me a
rare Psycho-Spiritual Experience.

In love,

Jacqueline

psyche's seeds

psyche's seeds

The Twelve Sacred Principles of Soul-Based Psychology

jacquelyn small

Jeremy P. Tarcher / Putnam
a member of Penguin Putnam Inc.
New York

Most Tarcher/Putnam books are available at special quantity
discounts for bulk purchases for sales promotions, premiums,
fund-raising, and educational needs. Special books or book excerpts
also can be created to fit specific needs. For details, write Putnam
Special Markets, 375 Hudson Street, New York, NY 10014.

Jeremy P. Tarcher/Putnam
a member of
Penguin Putnam Inc.
375 Hudson Street
New York, NY 10014
www.penguinputnam.com

Library of Congress Cataloging-in-Publication Data

Small, Jacquelyn.
Psyche's seeds : the twelve sacred principles of
soul-based psychology / Jacquelyn Small.
p. cm.
Includes index.
ISBN 1-58542-096-4
1. Spiritual life. 2. Cupid and Psyche (Tale). 3. Psychology,
Religious. I. Title.
BL624.S5946   2001   00-066759
291.4'4—dc21

Printed in the United States of America

1   3   5   7   9   10   8   6   4   2

This book is printed on acid-free paper ♾.

Book design by Chris Welch
Title page photo © Maura Rosenthal/Mspace

in appreciation . . .

To Brenda Rosen, my gifted editor and copilot for this inspired mission, whose brilliance and love for this project helped me ground the various themes of this heartfelt story into its final synthesis. Without your clarity, your depth of knowledge, and your willingness to keep my kaleidoscope brain on track, this book would never have made it from my heart to these pages. I am so grateful for our relationship and for its high calling.

To Tom Grady, my agent, whose continual belief in me and my vision of spiritual psychology keeps me visible as an author. Your guidance and support mean the world to me. I'm so fortunate to have you "in my corner."

To Mitch Horowitz and Joel Fotinos of Tarcher/Putnam for recognizing this vision and for your dedication to keeping timely, consciousness-raising books available to today's seekers of wisdom. I am honored to be a Tarcher author.

To Jeremy Tarcher for the vision you've consistently up-

in appreciation . . .

held in seeing that unknown talent and inspired writers have a way to get published. Thank you for bringing heart to this current technologically oriented world.

To my family, Mark, Brenda, Brett, Tom, and Michele, for your undying love for me and belief in what I stand for. You've always given me the support and freedom to pursue my dream.

And especially to Brenda Shea at the helm of Eupsychia's central office who keeps this living laboratory going in all its nitty-gritty detail, day by day.

To my senior staff and Eupsychia's interns, students, and all who participate in our workshop intensives, who've been the willing scientists of the soul who contribute their direct experience of how transformation really happens. This is your story, and I love you all!

While writing this book I fell in love, over and over, with Psyche and Eros for showing us the way, and with all of us for having the courage to participate in the greatest love story ever told—the marriage of the human with the Divine.

This book is dedicated to all seekers
of wisdom, beauty, and true love

contents

Introduction: Remembering Psyche 1

Seeds of My Awakening 15

The Love Story of Psyche and Eros 27

part I   psyche's four tasks 39

Beginning the Journey 41

  Task One Sorting the Seeds 51

  Task Two Gathering the Fleece 67

  Task Three Containing the Waters of Life 85

  Task Four Descending to the Underworld 105

part II   twelve seeds: thoughts for your journey   131

How to Use Psyche's Seeds   133

One You are both human and divine; only when both sides of
our nature are honored do we thrive.   137

Two The self is greater than its conditions.   146

Three What you say "I Am" to has a way of
claiming you.   155

Four The human shadow is not evil; it has
a sacred function.   166

Five Victimhood is a false concept that makes
you powerless.   176

Six Your desire nature is God's love manifesting
in your life.   186

Seven We learn to live within the tension of opposites
as walkers in two worlds.   198

Eight There can be no outer experts on a path of self-
knowledge; the learning comes from within.   208

Nine An open heart is the bridge to the Divine.   216

Ten Your symptoms of distress are not pathological; they are
the natural pangs of birthing a new consciousness.   225

Eleven Sacrifice is not a giving up but a taking on.   235

Twelve As you cultivate your own nature, all around you
begins to grow.   247

contents

Giving Birth to Joy   257

Spiritual Psychology Comes of Age   259

Epilogue: Becoming a Seed Bearer   265

Index   269

introduction

remembering psyche

This book is about the sacred purpose of being human and the journey we each must take to discover that purpose for ourselves. I've written it for all of you who are spiritual seekers, who are willing to explore the depths of the psyche to discover who you are and why you are here on earth.

The impulse to write this book started years ago when I realized how many people are desperately seeking a true spirituality. Many spiritual paths lead to the truth. Others, unfortunately, misguide us, because they ignore, or even violate, human nature. I am disturbed greatly by paths that teach that being human is sinful and that we must kill off the ego or step out of our humanness to be spiritual. My years of guiding people through the process of personal transformation during the healing intensives I've led have demonstrated to me the tragic dangers in this way of thinking—psychological ill health and, quite often, despair.

A healthy human psyche is the foundation upon which any authentic spiritual life is built. It is impossible to be "just spiritual," and there are no shortcuts on the path. Psychological healing goes hand-in-hand with spiritual awakening. There's no escaping it: *without a healthy psyche, we create a bogus spirituality.* Both psychological and spiritual principles must be honored for us to be healthy and whole.

In this book, you'll learn that you are both human and divine, a hybrid of matter and Spirit. And, like anything else in creation, you must honor the fundamental principles of your whole nature if you are to thrive. The principles of human nature transcend all philosophical and religious beliefs. If that nature is violated, like a hothouse violet in a snowstorm, you will wither and die.

Many believe that the human psyche is just mind—our psychological self whose issues can be worked out in therapy. But that's only half the story. In these pages, I offer a larger view of psyche: your psyche is your incarnated soul, the mirrored reflection of God or Spirit. Unfortunately, your psyche's mirror is often fogged by life wounds and other human distortions. Because psyche's mirror is not clear, it becomes the battlefield where conflicts between Spirit and matter play out. But psyche does not allow us to stay in misalignment with Spirit for long. It is relentless in bringing us the lessons in love we need to heal and be whole.

We begin our exploration of psyche's nature with the beautiful love story of Psyche and Eros, the ancient Greek tale of how a human girl marries a god and teaches him to love. As you follow Psyche's story, you experience her quest as she moves from innocence to wisdom through the four labors of love that she must complete to prepare herself to be the bride of a god. Along the way, you discover that when you make the decision to seek your true purpose and are willing to do deep inner work, Psyche is the archetype who becomes your guide. And, anytime you lose your inspiration, Eros is there to rekindle your fire.

When you've completed your journey with Psyche, the key principles of her story are laid out for you in the final section of the book in twelve Seed Thoughts. Each Seed Thought is a life lesson in psychological and spiritual wholeness. These ideas take root in your mind and help you ripen into a healthy spiritual life. I have seen for myself how powerful these principles are in my years of experiential work at Eupsychia, my national training program in spiritual psychology and psychospiritual integration. The word *eupsychia* means "psyche's well-being," and the principles underlying our work honor psyche's ways. I have taught these Seed Thoughts for years as the basic principles of psychospiritual integration. In writing this book I discovered, to my great delight, that these ideas track perfectly with the labors of love carried out by the mythical Psyche.

Before we begin the story, I want to reacquaint you with Psyche, since she's been left out of most spiritual teachings. I was shocked when I realized that Psyche had been overlooked—until I understood why. The reason we don't see Psyche or know much about her is because *we are her*. Standing in the middle of our own picture, we've not had a way to see ourselves; we've barely even made Psyche conscious.

If you think about it, you need a mirror to see your own face. Perhaps this is why Psyche came to earth, so that we can see through her that we are each reflections of Spirit.

So what is psyche? Your psyche is your inner life, the voice that speaks to you inside your head. Everything we think or feel comes through our psyches. Without psyche, we wouldn't be conscious of anything at all. Without psyche we'd be cut off from even knowing we are alive. Famed psychoanalyst Carl Gustav Jung said the human psyche gives us our knowledge of the world and the picture we make of it.

When we think of psyche, as the word is used today, we generally think of mind or consciousness—the root of the word *psychology*. But in its original Greek, *psyche* means "soul" and is associated with the breath or spirit of life that animates us from within. Psychology, truly understood, was to be the study of soul. Yet many psychologists focus on integrating the ego only. The deepest aim of a spiritual psychology is helping people reweave the threads that link mind and consciousness with soul and Spirit. Today, thank goodness, spiritual psychology is finally coming of age.

This book presents such a soul-based psychology, one that nourishes our spiritual nature as the underlying principle that guides the passionate earthly processes linked to ego and the material world. It points toward the principles that help us honor fully what it means to be human and so lay the foundation for true spirituality. The goal of soul-based psychology is to help us move beyond the belief that we would be happy if only we could resolve our doubts and fears and achieve the comfortable lifestyle, career, and relationship we think we need to feel good about ourselves. Spiritual psychology tells us, rather, that to be whole, the soul must express itself completely through every aspect of our life. It challenges us to understand that for us to heal, the shadow parts of our nature must be brought fully into consciousness. It helps us learn to live creatively from our center, guided by our unique sense of self—our inborn soul wisdom—rather than driven by the expectations of others or by society's unconscious drives to succeed.

You might be thinking that this path toward wholeness sounds like a lot of work, and you'd be right. Millions of people today are seeking to deepen their spiritual practice to find a way out of their problems. They try meditation or sign up for yoga classes or sit at the feet of one or another of the many spiritual teachers on the circuit because these paths seem to promise something practical that really works. Often they are disappointed and blame the teacher or the practice for the failure, certain that the next spiritual discipline they try on will be the right one.

These folk—and surely you can think of many people in your life who fit this description—are not mistaken in thinking that authentic spirituality is the answer to human suffering. But they are forgetting one thing. Since psyche gives rise to every thought and feeling, everything we know about the Divine and what it means to be spiritual also comes to us through psyche. It is impossible to be just spiritual, no matter how many hours we sit in meditation each day or how many spiritual disciplines we explore. We must first make conscious any of our perceptions that may be based in false beliefs. Unless we do our psychological homework, we risk using spiritual practice to escape into the high altitudes of denial where we can avoid taking care of sorely needed but uncomfortable unfinished personal business.

For example, as happens all too often in spiritual communities, an unhealed psyche might lead us to mistake the guru for the parent we never had and then blame the teacher for not fulfilling our unmet childhood needs. We have all heard stories about people with untreated romantic or sex addictions who act out their problems through inappropriately seductive behavior with a spiritual guide or a married fellow seeker. Or of people who were abused as children, who give their power over to a spiritual leader who is dogmatic or cruel, believing that self-destructive surrender is the only possible way to interact with a person in authority. A needy ego is how the shadow dances in all relationships. And when we're psychologically unclear, believe me, we find many willing partners! I've met people who call themselves spiritual who have closed hearts and glaring personal problems. Haven't you? We call this condition a spiritual bypass in our work, following the term coined by psychologist John Welwood.

In my work as a psychospiritual therapist, teacher, and writer, I have watched and assisted hundreds of people as they move through the process of healing wounds like these. Some of their stories will be told in what follows. This work has taught me an important truth: only by merging our quest for psychological health with our spiritual intent—a process I call psychospiritual integration—can our deeply ingrained, dysfunctional patterns be transformed.

Our unresolved fears and needs for power trick us into false beliefs that actually lead to more suffering. Some caught in this way might decide that being spiritual means they must always be positive and loving. Others, that the particular path to Spirit they are following is the only path, or that their charismatic teacher is the only teacher worth listening to. I think of these people as trapped in their unhealed original wounds and contaminating Spirit with their complexes and neuroses. If our psyches retain seeds of disturbance left over from personal trauma or from unconscious beliefs we've adopted, we may fall prey to false teachers or wind up on a path that is glamorous but flawed. A premature transcendence is no transcendence at all. Illusions always eventually fail us.

Psyche teaches us what it means to be human and grounds us in experience before we go launching into the airy worlds of Spirit. When we make psyche our study, our focus shifts from trying to *leave* life to *living* life more consciously. When it does, we notice that treasures of spiritual wisdom start pouring through our personality in ordinary human ways.

To our delight, we discover that the side of us that is our flawed and suffering human self is also divine. Integrating this revelation fully heals us and makes us whole—in fact, it's the only thing that can!

So who is this mysterious Psyche?

Psyche's nature and qualities will unfold more fully as we explore her story, but as a beginning we might say that Psyche is our incarnated soul—the part of our being that expresses the individual essence or unique flavor of who we are.

The most interesting thing about Psyche is that she is both human and divine. The same soul that makes us human and individual also links us to Spirit. Psyche, I like to say, looks both ways. When she looks downward, toward earth, she interpenetrates the human experience and infuses it with Spirit's ways, but when she looks upward, toward heaven, she participates in the Spiritual Soul that is the breath of the Divine and makes our humanness a gift to Spirit, so that we become united with the One Soul of all there is.

Psyche, we might say, is a dynamic relationship. She mediates between Spirit and matter, between Everything and the unique, individual self that we experience ourselves to be, between personal and transpersonal life. As a mirrored reflection of the Spiritual Soul that manifests in each of us, Psyche's task is to take on fully the human predicament, with all its problems and shadows, and guide us on a journey, the goal of which is bringing our human soul back into alignment with the Divine.

Because your psyche can look both ways, she is linked both to our individual human mind and to all-knowing Divine Consciousness. We catch sight of this aspect of our psyche's two-way vision when her mirror is unclouded and she surprises us with a flash of intuition or a numinous inner vision, one of those divinely inspired insights or mystical experiences—I call them Soul Events—that come to us seemingly out of nowhere when we are ready to grow or change.

A Soul Event is a pure revelation that comes straight from

Source, which brings us an instantaneous knowing that we are divine. When such a profound inner experience comes to us, there is nothing we need to process or interpret. Our learning is direct and immediate. Sometimes such revelations come to us in clumps. A book falls from the shelf and opens to a page that validates exactly what was on our mind. We meet a significant friend or teacher at just the right moment and it changes our life. An unexpected trip forces us to detour from the comfortable track we were following and move in a new direction. An auto accident or illness jolts us out of ordinary reality for a timeless moment and unveils our bigger story. A meditation session or dream opens into a mystical vision that unfolds another chapter in our life's true path. I've noticed that all Soul Events are connected, though at times long fallow stretches, years perhaps, intervene between these high reminders. I believe Soul Events come to us from the world of eternal reality and are timed according to the psyche's idea of when we need them to remember who we are.

Now, you may be wondering why I am referring to the psyche as *she* and asking yourself whether men's souls are feminine too. The answer is yes, but you must also remember that women's souls have a masculine aspect as well. The male and female I am speaking of here have nothing to do with gender. Rather they are the objective and subjective principles, the yang and yin of Chinese philosophy, or animus and anima of depth psychology, out of which rise the dynamic tension that gifts our soul with energy and creativity.

psyche's seeds

The Psyche that I speak of is feminine for another reason as well. Psyche figures in one of the most beautiful and significant love stories of the ancient world, first recorded in *The Golden Ass* by Apuleius in the second century A.D. The myth Apuleius tells will feel familiar, as it is the origin of many of the characters and motifs of the fairy tales we know.

Why do myths fascinate us so? Perhaps it is because myths speak in symbol and metaphor of both the archetypal origins of the universal human story and of the life experiences of every individual. Myths show us our personal problems through new eyes and help us to remember that our issues are everyone's issues. Moreover, myths reveal truths that are often the unconscious motivators of our feelings and behaviors. The characters of myth, archetypes like Psyche and Eros, are "real" in that they function within the human psyche and change us. As psychic impulses, archetypes drive our inner human unfolding and inspire us toward our highest ideals.

When you embark upon a mythical odyssey, such as you'll find in these pages, you are following in the footsteps of those who have gone before, travelers who have left markers along the way to assist us on our journey of awakening. These deep promptings gratify our souls, since we love to hear of the divine world drama in which we all play a part. Our own life story is the latest chapter of any myth's unfolding, as I will remind you from time to time as we progress.

At its most profound level, then, the myth of Psyche is a spiritual parable of the transformational journey we all go through to regain the memory that we are divine, and so become complete. As the archetype of the human soul, Psyche's journey through incarnation teaches us of our soul's longing to be human and of our human longing for spiritual transcendence. At the intersection of these two yearnings, the world comes into being. The nineteenth-century Russian poet Daniel Chwolsohn, in Die Ssabier und der Ssabismus, *volume II*, expresses beautifully the emotion of this mystical truth:

> *The soul once turned toward matter, fell in love with it,*
> *and burning with desire to experience bodily pleasures,*
> *was no longer willing to tear herself away from it.*
> *So was the world born.*

As this book unfolds, Psyche's story will be told and interpreted in detail. Psyche is the goddess who chose to become a mortal and to experience the fall from Mt. Olympus, the home of the gods. While on earth, Psyche forgot her goddess nature and believed she was only human, just as we all have done.

Psyche's journey through incarnation, which culminates in her marriage to a god, has much to teach us about our personal quest for psychological and spiritual wholeness. This quest follows what I call the path of direct experience. It is a harrowing journey, full of peril and promise, mysterious helpers, miraculous insights, tricks and stratagems, despair and victory. Seen rightly, it is our journey, for all men and women embody both Psyche and Eros. *Psyche's Seeds* may make you conscious of this fact for the first time. And if so, you may expect more magic to start happening in your life rather quickly. For the recognition of an archetype is what activates it in your psyche.

Fortunately for us, the road Psyche travels toward full consciousness is mapped, though not in the ordinary way. We might think of the path of personal growth in fairy-tale fashion as a spiraling track marked by a trail of seeds scattered along its twists and turns. If we pay attention, these subtle signs keep us on course, pointed in the right direction. In my workshops and healing intensives, I have seen that though the twistings and turnings of each person's journey are unique, most people on a path of transformation pass similar markers. To the extent that we can be conscious travelers, looking carefully to spot the seeds of wisdom that appear at significant turnings in the road, we can make rapid progress.

I call these road markers Seed Thoughts—divine ideas pregnant with living truth that take root in your mind and transform your life. As you read these Seed Thoughts and the stories of people who have passed through these points on their journeys, some will seem very familiar and remind you of similar passages in your own life. Others may not speak to you yet, but might become important down the road as your personal journey unfolds.

At the end of the journey, like Psyche of the myth, we arrive at a place we only dreamed of—grown into the fulfilled, soul-blessed Divine Self we are meant to become. In the end, Psyche becomes not only the bride of a god but a goddess herself. Could this transformation be our sacred mission as well? Is our reason for living to journey toward being more godlike while simultaneously we allow the gods, through us, to experience being human? If so, the blend of psychological health and spiritual qualities that Psyche's story can teach us may be the key to fulfillment, not only for ourselves but for our world.

We are all part of a great world drama the deep purpose of which is to allow the Spiritual Soul to come to light in this world. The need of the world at any given time will play its part in conditioning the human psyche: And when our mirror is clear and the Spirit's impulse can shine through, there will be a personal response that meets the collective need. We play our part by bringing a godlike delight into our human personal relationships. When we do, the passionate ego and the light-filled soul become one. In mythic terms, we marry our souls to love and give birth, as Psyche does when she is united with Eros, to a child named Joy.

seeds of my awakening

My own life journey has certainly had its twists and turns. Looking back, I often wish someone had scattered some helpful seeds along the track for me to follow when the going got rough and confusing. Yet, in a way, Someone did. In sharing with you these seeds of my own awakening, I'm inviting you to recall your own. I am convinced that Soul Events such as I have experienced happen to us all and are for the purpose of marking the Spiritual Soul's promptings to awaken us to love. Unfortunately, we usually only learn about real love from experiencing unlove, or from taking troublesome turns in life that wind up as painful lessons. When we can see the deeper meaning of a difficulty, its significance for our soul's growth, this is transformative; we are seeing through the eyes of our soul. When we choose to struggle through an issue consciously, keenly watching every aspect of it as we engage, our life energies accumulate in the deeper strata of our psyches so that an archetypal healing can come through. Once something is seen all the way to its archetypal significance, it is finished. The issue will vanish from our lives, no longer commanding any of our precious energy.

As you read along, reflect upon any "big dreams," visions, revelations, or visits from inner spiritual guides you've remembered. These are all messages from your soul. Your soul's timeless life is unfolding upon a larger canvas, and each peak experience that we recall is just one more chapter in our one unfolding greater story.

Since I was very small, I have always had the sense of being guided from within, of Someone talking to me from inside my head who was always loving and never judged me. I felt sometimes as if I were onstage, that Someone was watching over me, protecting me, keeping me on course. This Someone rarely paid me compliments, but I knew I was cherished no matter what I did. Since I never wanted to disappoint my inner guide, I was always spurred on to do my best. My inner guide wore a brown monk's robe, but I never saw his face. I knew he was from another world and no part of my regular life. His voice gave no hint of the inner critic who sometimes shames us, such as an internalized parental figure or formidable teacher.

I have since come to understand that this inner voice speaks the promptings of our souls, and that its function is to remind us, again and again, that no matter how complicated and confusing the details of our human journey, our soul is journeying with us. Because our human journey is also a soul journey, divine guidance and inspiration are always available, if we can only tune in to the Someone within. This Someone—our soul—is always urging us forward, for Psyche cannot rest until she has accomplished her earthly tasks, until a new self is fashioned out of her trials and pains, until she—and we—are whole.

It's an interesting exercise, and rather comforting, really, to look back over one's life and see it as the soul's story, to see its ups and downs as a series of trials we had to undergo and impossible tasks we needed to fulfill in order to guide our soul along the path toward completion. Viewed this way, our most painful moments have been our greatest teachers, when seeds have been sown in our psyches that blossom into emotional and spiritual maturity. This bird's-eye perspective is difficult to hold when we're in the midst of troubles, but looking back, we can often see evidence of the seeds of our own awakening being laid down.

My seeds have often been sown by children—living children and dying ones. This pattern got started by my own difficult birth as a tiny four-pound, seven-month preemie coming into the world in a rural Texas hospital without proper incubators. I would have died but for a kindly doctor who devised an incubator for me—an open oven door in his own kitchen!

I once relived this experience in a therapeutic rebirthing session. The rebirthing coach who was working with me tells me that as I experienced the events of my birth, I cried out "I miss my father" and "No one here knows how to feed me." It seems clear to me now that these cries had a deeper meaning—that from my soul's perspective, the father I was missing was my heavenly Father, and the nourishment I feared I would not find was spiritual food. This memory helps me make sense of the feeling I have carried with me always of having come into this life with the timing all wrong and with no instruction book. It reminds me that events in this life function on multiple levels, as episodes in our personal biography and as markers on our psychic or soul journey.

The births and deaths of my own children have underscored this teaching for me. My firstborn son nearly died at two and a half from undiagnosed juvenile diabetes. After the birth of a healthy daughter, I miscarried two subsequent babies, nearly dying of a hemorrhage during the second. I also carried to full term and delivered a baby who had died in my womb during my fifth month of pregnancy. Eventually I did have another child, a second son, who was, fortunately, completely healthy.

At the human level, these tragedies nearly undid me. As an only child who had seldom been around small children, no mother could have been less prepared than I was for the impossible task of administering three insulin injections a day and precisely weighing and measuring every morsel of food my child put into his mouth, for this was what it took to keep him alive. Yet this exacting task became a lifeline for me and kept me going through the births and deaths of my other children. When I nearly bled to death in my hospital bed during my second miscarriage, I had a clear sense of leaving my body, entering the body of my eight-year-old diabetic son, and being told that my mother had died. The sharp pang I felt in my/his heart propelled me back into my own body, where the intervention of my doctor saved my life.

Near-death experiences are, for many of us, unforgettable Soul Events that change us forever. My diabetic son had several such experiences, which were also important soul lessons for me. One in particular stands out. My son had been in the hospital yet again with a kidney condition that I was told might be fatal. I was numb with fright. While he was recovering, I went to a therapeutic breath work retreat at Esalen in California. As I engaged in the deep breathing process, I was aware that I was grieving the feared loss of my son. I clutched my stomach where the energy seemed to be compressed and cried quietly in self-pity, "Why me? Why him?"

Then, suddenly, I felt the compressed energy release and fly up through my heart and out my head. I seemed to be soaring through the sky, seeing at once all the mothers in the world who had sick or dying children: mothers in India holding starving babies to their breasts, mothers on their knees next to hospital beds praying that a child would live, mothers holding a telegram telling them that a son had been wounded or killed in battle. Inside my head, I heard the words, *This, too, is just another human experience.*

When the vision ended and I came back to myself, I knew that I was not alone, that mothers everywhere have lived through experiences similar to mine. Linked now to the grief and fear of all mothers who have lost children, I felt the strength to bear it, just as they had. Much later, I learned from my training with medical researcher Stanislav Grof that when we gain access to the archetypal level of a personal issue and recognize its universal significance, our personal pain will heal. Connected to all the grieving mothers in the world, I was no longer filled with pity for myself.

Looked at from the soul's bird's-eye view, human trials always take on a deeper significance. Soul unfolds in our inner lives upon a larger canvas, undergoing rites of passage and initiations that carry it forward on its timeless evolutionary journey. Sometimes while we are going through a soul-mediated experience, we are unable to fathom its purpose. Only in retrospect does its meaning become clear. At the time when I delivered my stillborn baby, for instance, I wasn't able to integrate the experience, so I repressed much of my sorrow. Years later, in a rebirthing session, I found myself reliving this event. In a meditative state, I saw an image of my dead baby as if it were lying on the left-hand side of a triangle. On the right-hand side, light was bouncing around. As I watched, the light kept flying over to the dark, dead side, gradually filling it with light. When the dark side was fully illuminated, I saw, at the top of the triangle, a Divine Child in a healthy womb, awaiting rebirth! The message of my vision was clear: death is an illusion. From the perspective of the deep psyche, I had given birth not to a stillborn but to a Divine Child, who is, at the soul level, immortal, and always rebirthing, as is every living being.

The mingling of birth and death in my life has taught my soul its most significant lesson: birth and death are two sides of a single coin whose name is transformation. At every moment of seeming death, new life is always coming into being. Whenever something in our life is dying, we can take comfort from the thought that something new is also being born; a rebirth is waiting, just around the corner of our awareness. It's no wonder that I've wound up guiding people through the death/rebirth stages of transformation!

For women especially, the births and deaths of intimate relationships are another way this lesson is brought home. This is certainly true for me. Like Psyche of the myth, I married for the first time as a teenager, choosing a partner in the darkness of preconscious immaturity for all the reasons a teenager would fall in love. In my innocence, I married my youthful husband because he was strikingly handsome and a baseball star! But we were wrong for each other in every way important to our soul's unfoldment.

My second marriage was flawed in a different way. My husband was a strong and powerful leader, an established attorney who became a U.S. Circuit Court judge. I was awash in wealth and privilege. One Christmas, my mother-in-law gave me twenty-six pairs of shoes from Neiman-Marcus! I never even opened all the boxes. Our four-story Georgian home was filled with fine antiques and our evenings with a mad whirl of dinner parties and social galas.

Despite all this, I was miserable. Much as I tried to derive a sense of being someone from my connection to such a dynamic husband, it was not enough. My soul demanded that I become someone of value in my own right. One evening while entertaining a huge crowd of people in our home, I broke into hysterical laughter, shattering a cut-glass punch cup right in the middle of a solemn video of one of our guests' trek through England. That night, I knew it was over. I was surrounded by deadness, feeling that nothing in my life had meaning. This marriage, too, was wrong for my soul's true purpose, but another great lesson had been learned.

I have come to understand that what we experience as falling in love is often prompted by strong attractions we don't fully understand. Though we may try to resist the magnetic pull of a person who may be clearly wrong for us, I have seen again and again that this is nearly impossible. Generally we are powerless to resist the magnetism of romantic love that draws us toward someone, no matter how inappropriate the pairing. Seen in the light of the soul's journey, the intensity of our desire nature makes better sense. Perhaps in each attraction is either a needed lesson or a true soul expression seeking to manifest.

If the attraction leads to a way our soul can express, we are obviously delighted and will feel right on track. If one leads to a painful lesson, we go through a process that, ideally, will teach us what illusion caught us unawares, or show us a quality we still lack. If we make the lesson conscious, we will grow. Either way can be the workings of the soul, who always wants our greatest good. Perhaps all of these "little loves" are aspects of the one Beloved that we know in our hearts to be our other half, the missing part that completes us and makes us a whole self. The self, as I have said, contains both masculine and feminine principles. Bringing these two halves together makes us feel complete. Each earthly union in which we engage, no matter how disastrous in human terms, is an approximation of this goal and contributes something toward the soul's unfoldment. The love story of Psyche and Eros, as you will see, is a mythic retelling of this union of our two "halves."

Of course it's hard to remember the soul level of the story when your human heart is breaking. The ending of my third marriage nearly killed me. In a Chinese restaurant over egg rolls and cashew chicken, my beloved husband calmly ended what was for me still a passionate love match. I returned home and lay across the bed in a stupor, feeling that my life was over. I didn't have the courage to kill myself, so I pleaded with God just to take me away. I hoped if I lay there quietly enough, I'd fade out as I nearly had in the hospital when I was hemorrhaging. I was so humiliated, I couldn't imagine getting out of bed again. I hated men. And I hated myself.

Suddenly, as I lay there, I heard a powerful and familiar voice speaking inside my head. The Someone of my childhood was ordering me to get up, go into my study, and read *Discipleship in the New Age*, volume I, page 146. It was that specific. This was a book I owned but had never read. I thought I was having an auditory hallucination. *Maybe this is how death happens*, I said to myself. But I got up and did as the voice suggested.

There on the page were words that pointed beyond my current despair to a new birth, reminding me of my real purpose for being here. In unequivocal terms, I was being told that I needed to "acquire an increased ability to voice truth through the medium of the written word" so that I could write a book that would reach the thinkers of the world with new ideas in the field of psychology. This book, the passage went on, "must be wrought out in the crucible of energetic living and must not be a product of seclusion."

Though these words had been written in the 1930s to someone else, I knew this message was for me. At that moment, standing there in my study, my third marriage in shambles, I stepped solidly onto my path. My life's work began to unfold before me, urging me back into the crucible of energetic living. The book I wrote inspired by this experience, *Transformers: The Artists of Self-Creation* expresses so much more than my mind understood at that time. It was truly soul work that flowed from Psyche in union with Eros, deep inside.

Not long after this experience, I had a "big dream"—one with transpersonal significance—that seemed to validate my personal mission. In the dream, I was walking along the main street of a small town lined with stalls in which people were living. It looked a little like the stage set for an old TV Western. I was going door to door, inviting people to come out and look at the beautiful vista I'd seen from the cliff at the edge of town. From that vantage point, I had gazed upon a beautiful new world, filled with everything anyone had ever dreamed life could be. The vision was numinous and compelling. As each door opened, I announced this good news. Each time I was given an excuse why the family couldn't get away. One family had a relative with a broken finger. Another had too many children. Another had a sick dog. Finally I gave up. All alone, I walked to the edge of the cliff and sat down, looking wistfully at the new world. No one, I realized sadly, understood; no one would come. They needed more preparation, some kind of bridge into the new world.

When I woke up, I knew this dream was another reminder of my life's work. I was to be a messenger, a Pied Piper who would lead people to their growing edge and invite them to expand beyond their limitations. And during the next four years while writing the book *Transformers*, another vision came, which was published at the beginning of the book. I had seen a large ship float down from the sky and hover above the ocean. Invisible hands threw down a rope ladder that barely reached the surface of the water. The ladder had six rungs. A seventh disappeared onto the deck of the ship. Hundreds of people were swimming toward the ship. Some were happily climbing the ladder. Others were ignoring the ship completely, swimming here and there; still others were drowning or already dead. I named this vehicle of transformation the *Mother Ship*. I knew she had come for all of us.

Where will she take us? To Infinity, our true home. Once in a deep meditative state where my visionary imagination ignited, I saw what Infinity might be like. I was with several brother and sister souls lying casually on our sides, with our heads propped on our arms, looking down at the earth as we turned slowly on some kind of rotating wheel—perhaps the Wheel of Fate. As we watched various earth scenes unfold, we talked about which roles we might "dive into" and play out for one another. "You be Farmer Brown, and I will be your wife," I said to a brother soul. "I'll be your enemy in this life and bring you down. This will help you grow," another soul said to me. From the perspective of Infinity, we were perfect and nonattached. We could see clearly the archetypal dimension of every human story and its sacred purpose. This poignant vision taught me that the soul is most content in a godlike state. Incarnation in a human body is constricting. Perhaps you can relate to this sense. Many people have told me that they sometimes feel as if they want to burst out of their skins and return to the All from which they came.

It is so easy to discount these vignettes of our higher life when they appear. If you will keep a journal and write down your dreams or any significant visions that you have, you will invite your soul's unfolding life to be revealed to you more often. Soul Events need only to be recognized to become a reality.

That journey home is the story that this book tells. You will see that it is a very human story, full of grief and struggle, mistakes and betrayals. Like the story line of any life, my own included, it asks us to believe that the soul's unfolding will bring each of us the work, the opportunities, even the partners and co-workers we need to fulfill our divine purpose. It demonstrates without question, as I have discovered for myself, that anytime we really need help, we have only to turn within, for Someone is always there to guide us.

the love story of
psyche and eros

I have always loved the story of Psyche and Eros. Whenever I tell Psyche's story in a seminar or workshop, my listeners are transfixed, and I am moved anew by this magical tale that speaks so eloquently to the heart of everyone who has ever loved and lost and found love again.

Yet the real power of the myth comes not from its fairy tale characters and story line but from the message of hope it gives us that genuine transformation is possible. On its deepest level, this thrilling love story reminds us that every human soul comes into mortal form from the realm of the gods, journeys through life to grow into fully conscious maturity, a journey from innocence to wisdom, and in the end, winds its way to joyous fulfillment.

Psyche began her life as a goddess on Mt. Olympus, adored by the gods for her beauty and purity. So enamored did Psyche become of the homage paid to her beauty that she forgot her immortal nature and fell to earth, reborn as a mortal. Some say she was conceived by dewdrops that fell from the sky, an image that reminds us that each individual soul or psyche is also a divine dewdrop, precipitating from the one Spiritual Soul.

In her human incarnation, Psyche was the youngest of three lovely daughters of a king and queen. The worshipful attention she had enjoyed in the immortal realms increased a thousandfold on earth. Apuleius tells us that every day, her father's subjects came to gaze on Psyche's beauty, blowing kisses to her and scattering rose garlands in her path. As the fame of Psyche's beauty spread, her admirers neglected the shrines and festivals of Aphrodite, worshipping instead the mortal Psyche.

But Psyche, unconscious of her divine power, drew no satisfaction from these honors. Her preconscious state mirrors our innocence at the beginning of our journey toward self-realization. In our immaturity, we often overidentify with some larger-than-life ideal—parent, teacher, spouse, god or goddess, as Psyche is overidentified with Aphrodite—from whose reflected glory we borrow a sense of our own identity. Yet this false self gives us no genuine satisfaction, as the boundaries between the self-sense we have borrowed and the greater other with whom we identify are blurred and murky. In Jungian psychology, this undifferentiated state is called the participation mystique, a closed circle of connection in which we are inextricably trapped in some process of unconscious living. I experienced this condition in my unhappy second marriage, when I tried to base my sense of self on my prestigious husband's identity. I was participating in being married in an unconscious stereotyped manner, not yet awakened to the fact that I was a unique individual woman. Without knowing who we are in our own right, we cannot relate authentically to another, as Psyche also discovers. Though everyone marveled at Psyche's beauty, no mortal man dared to woo her, leaving her lonely and miserable.

Aphrodite, ancient goddess of love and beauty, was enraged that her rightful homage was being usurped by a mere mortal. Since mythic characters are humankind's archetypes, every character represents an aspect of ourselves. So just as we are, in many ways, the preconscious Psyche, we are also Aphrodite. As the archetype of the Divine Feminine, Aphrodite is an aspect of the soul of every man and woman. This essential part of our inner nature may well be enraged at being unrecognized and dishonored by our unthinking preoccupation with the merely human level of our life story. Aphrodite's schemes and stratagems are universal, not personal, designed to make Psyche—and us—pay attention to our Divine Feminine self, which we regularly neglect and ignore.

Psyche's parents, despairing that Psyche was still unmarried despite her great beauty, asked the oracle of Apollo where to find a husband for their daughter. Apollo replied that Psyche should be taken to the top of a mountain, chained to a rock, and abandoned. There she would be married to the most dreadful monster Hades, the god of death. There was no resisting the oracle's commands. Psyche's wedding procession was also her funeral march, and the beautiful Psyche, resolute though weeping and trembling, was left alone in the dark to await her terrible fate.

In some ways, for women especially and for many men as well, marriage is a kind of death or profound transformation. It represents the end of innocence and the beginning of adult cares and responsibilities. Often, however, though we may wish for marriage to grow us up, it does not do so. My youthful first marriage could not transport me instantly into adulthood, perhaps because my husband and I were not mature enough spiritually even to be aware that marriage has a soul level.

A true marriage is a mystical merging of personality and soul that happens energetically. It is an outward reflection of the inner reunion of the masculine and feminine halves of our nature into the One from which all duality arises. Both the man and the woman in such a pairing must be willing to sacrifice something of their own identity to create a greater whole. Psyche's self-sacrifice on the mountaintop— the word *sacrifice* actually means "to make holy"—was preconscious. She was truly in the dark, with no identity of her own to give up, only the reflected glory of her Aphrodite-like beauty. Though she willingly abandoned herself to her fate, it would take much more than dying to her girlhood to make Psyche's soul grow up in this human world.

Jealous Aphrodite, who had been watching the drama unfold on the mountaintop, called her son Eros, or Cupid, to her side. It was typical of Aphrodite to use her son/lover Eros as her agent for sowing passion in the human world. As a universal archetype, Aphrodite knows little of personal love, having never experienced it herself. To revenge the slights to her divinity, she instructed Eros to wound Psyche with one of his arrows so that she would fall in love with any dreadful creature who would come to claim her as his bride. Eros, also preconscious and under the sway of his powerful mother, did as he was told. But as he drew an arrow from his quiver, he pricked his own finger on its tip and fell in love with the lovely girl. Eros, adept at making others fall in love, had never felt love's potent sting himself until now!

So who, we must ask, is Eros? On one level, Eros is the male in every romantic relationship, the masculine energy that joins in perfect union with feminine energy in the sacred dimension of every human pairing. As the masculine principle, or animus, within the soul of every man and woman, Eros dances in each of us in dynamic tension with the anima, or feminine principle. The thrust of erotic energy is outward. Linked to sexuality and the human will, Eros, as the spirit seed of inspiration, motivates us with arrows of attraction to seek out people and experiences that contribute to our soul growth.

In depth psychology, Eros is also the archetype of passionate love. When the Eros principle is lacking in us, nothing interests us. We lack passion for work and play, as well as for loving relationships with others. Our inner Eros calls us back to a state before we were divided against ourselves— head from heart, masculine reason from feminine intuition. In the state of wholeness to which Eros invites us, we are in love with the whole world!

Yet in the Psyche myth, Eros, too, had learning to do. Psychologically immature himself, Eros wished to remain eternally youthful. He is the archetype of the *puer aeternus*, the eternal youth, still cloaked in his mother's adoration, who shrinks from knowledge and responsibility. Like Psyche, Eros was content to remain in the dark, to seek whimsical pleasure without accountability, coupling without commitment.

We can see this aspect of Eros acted out when he fell in love with Psyche. Rather than approach her directly, Eros sent the West Wind to lift Psyche from her mountaintop and waft her gently to a lovely valley, where she fell asleep on a bed of soft turf sprinkled with flowers. When she awoke, her fears somewhat allayed, Psyche made her way through the forest until she came to an exquisite palace with silver walls and a jeweled floor and invisible servants who supplied her with delicious refreshments, a luxurious bath, and royal garments to wear. After a sumptuous banquet during which she was serenaded by an unseen choir, Psyche was led to a splendid bedchamber, undressed by invisible hands, and helped into her marriage bed.

For a long time Psyche lay awake in the dark, her fears returning. Toward midnight, she heard a gentle voice whispering in her ear. It was her unknown husband come to claim her. Now he was climbing into her bed. Now he was taking her into his arms and making her his wife. Before dawn broke, he left her, making only one request. "Dearest wife," he told her, "living here in my palace you will have everything you desire, and each night I will come to you in our bed. But promise me that you will not ask to see my face or know anything more about me. Only then can we remain together in this paradise." Psyche agreed and promised to abide by her husband's strange request. In her innocence, Psyche chose to live in the night world of the unconscious rather than insisting that the personal love she and her husband shared be brought openly into the light of conscious awareness.

The youthful coupling of Psyche and Eros is not unlike the early stages of many marriages or romantic relationships. Like the prince and princess of many fairy tales, Eros and Psyche would seem to have everything they need to live happily ever after—as do we all when we remain in a dreamlike state of ideal love. Like many a modern princess, however—myself included—happily ever after can only last so long. Then the soul demands that we seek growth and evolution, that we break the chains of comfortable confinement—whether within an enchanted palace or a stately Georgian home—and move forward on our quest for our deeper destiny.

The instrument of our growth out of our childish paradise is often a shadow aspect of our nature. As depth psychology explains, the shadow is the dark, unknown side of our personality—the qualities and tendencies we are ashamed of and deny having, even to ourselves, because they undercut our ego's comfortable notion of who we are. Often we do not know our shadow until we meet someone who pushes our buttons, who makes us unreasonably furious or miserable or who we are sure is entirely to blame for something that is troubling us. When our negative reaction to someone is disproportionately strong, we are often recoiling from the unsettling sight of a piece of our shadow reflected in the mirror of another person. If we stop for a moment and ask ourselves, "What part of my own nature am I seeing in this person?" we often find that we have owned a piece of our shadow and reeled in a hidden part of ourselves that we projected onto someone else.

At the soul level, shadow work is even more important. Anything that remains unconscious in us has the power to ruin us, as Psyche soon discovers. As we shine the light of awareness on the unhealed, unredeemed parts of our spiritual being, we begin to learn the quality of spiritual discrimination—the ability to separate the essentials and nonessentials in our lives and the willingness to heal or walk away from what's blocking our soul's development. Shadow work is sacred work. It engenders our compassion for others and our compassion for ourselves. The human shadow is the holy grit that forces us to move toward the realization of our soul's ideal.

In the Psyche myth, the role of the shadow is enacted by Psyche's two elder sisters. Word had reached them that Psyche was living in a beautiful palace full of treasures with a god as her husband. Their jealousy aroused, they decided to seek out the truth of these stories and see if there could be some benefit to themselves in Psyche's situation. Leaving their homes, the sisters climbed to the mountaintop where Psyche was last seen and called out her name. Down in the valley, Psyche heard her sisters' cries and, mistaking their envy for grief at her supposed death, begged her husband to command the West Wind to carry her sisters down to the valley to visit her so that she could reassure them that she was well.

Eros warned Psyche that her sisters were a danger to their love, and begged her to ignore their cries. But Psyche was adamant. She refused to eat and spent her days weeping for her sisters. At last, Eros relented. "But keep your promise and say nothing to your sisters about me. Be faithful, Psyche, and our child, which is even now growing in your womb, will be born immortal and a god. Break your faith, and our child will be mortal." Psyche promised, thrilled at the news that she was carrying her beloved's child.

When her sisters arrived, Psyche fell on them with tears and greetings. Then she showed her sisters the wonders of the palace and showered them with lavish gifts, which only inflamed their jealousy further. The sisters bombarded Psyche with questions about her husband. "Who is he?" they demanded, "What does he look like? How did he come by such riches?" Poor Psyche tried one explanation after another. Her husband was a rich merchant away on a voyage, a hunter on a trek in the forest, a prince in disguise. Understood in psychological terms, these tales were fictions with which Psyche was comforting herself, and her sisters' insistence on knowing the real story was the shadow of her own need for certainty. In the end, she told her sisters the truth, that she had never seen her husband, as he came to her only in the dark of night.

Determined to reveal the secret and seize Psyche's wealth for themselves, the sisters devised a plan. Feigning worry for Psyche's well-being, they reminded her that the oracle of Apollo had professed that she would be married to a loathsome monster. "Your husband," they told her, "is a serpent or other terrible beast. He is waiting until your womb is full and your child ready to be born. Then he plans to devour you both!" In great detail, the sisters explained what Psyche must do to protect herself. She was, they said, to hide a sharp knife and an oil lamp behind a curtain near her bed. When her beast/husband was sleeping, she must light the lamp and use the knife to kill the monster that was revealed by its glow.

Poor Psyche was torn but terrified. She loved her husband, but believed her sisters, whose words reflected back her own misgivings and shadowy fears. No longer content to remain unconscious, Psyche gathered the things her sisters suggested and prepared to betray her marriage vow.

That night, when her husband was asleep, she crept out of bed, grasped the knife, and uncovered the lamp. But instead of a fearful monster, the lamp's soft radiance revealed the beautiful face of a sleeping god. Shaken and guilt stricken, Psyche stumbled backward, pricking her own finger on an arrow in the quiver belonging to her husband that hung at the side of the bed and spilling a drop of hot oil from the lamp onto her husband's shoulder. This moment is the key to the psychological meaning of the myth: a young woman individuates—births a separate and mature self—by bringing her feelings of love into the light of consciousness.

In myth, oil symbolizes the loving reverence given to a being thought to be greater than oneself, as modeled by Mary Magdalene when she anointed Jesus' feet. When Psyche shined the light on Eros, she was making their love conscious and saw her divine lover in all his godlike glory. Because he was unwilling to be a conscious god, still in his youthful narcissistic stage, the lamp's oil wounded him rather than anointing him, causing him to flee to his mother. This is typical behavior for a *puer aeternus*, a male who wishes to remain a youth.

Experiencing the penetrating burn from the hot oil, Eros awoke with a start and understood immediately what had happened. Sadly, he unwound Psyche's arms from around his neck and, without a word, flew off to Olympus, leaving Psyche, wounded now for the first time by love's arrow, weeping inconsolably on the ground.

The path of love is central to a woman's psychospiritual unfolding. Conscious love not only illumines a woman and moves her closer to her mate but eventually helps the man grow into maturity as well, as we will see happens to Eros in the future when his narcissistic wound is healed. Interestingly, it is Psyche's *humanness* that is inviting a god to love. Eros had never felt love himself; he only knew impersonally how to cause others to fall in love, often irresponsibly.

How often in our lives do we contrive somehow to upset our own apple cart? To participate, perhaps unconsciously, in events that force us to grow beyond an outmoded way of living? Perhaps it's by falling in love with the wrong person. Perhaps it's by ignoring a warning or betraying a secret or breaking a promise. Often it is a kind of disobedience that pushes us toward awakening. When our soul decrees that it is time to grow, no contrary arguments or logical misgivings can dissuade us. We must uncover our lamp and shine the light of consciousness into the shadowy corners of our lives and, come what may, embark on the often harrowing journey toward psychological and spiritual maturity.

Psyche could not be genuinely happy in a paradise based on ignorance. Seen in its larger, soul sense, her betrayal of her husband was the highest fidelity to her own truth—the truth that only by seeing ourselves and others clearly can we begin the work of refining our souls to do the work of Spirit. Her innocence now shattered, Psyche must embark on the difficult path to wisdom, which can only be gained through one's own direct experience, the quest for transformation that is the soul's only way home.

In the next part of the book, we look in detail at the four tasks, the labors of love Psyche must complete in order to reunite with Eros, the "other half" of her soul. As we will see, Psyche's quest for Eros is reflected in our lives on two levels. Like Psyche, many of us are searching for personal love, for the life partner who, we feel, will make our existence complete. On the inner level, however, Psyche's quest—and ours—is for ways to bring together the inner masculine and inner feminine, which are necessary and complementary aspects of psychic wholeness.

The sense that many of us have of being split apart comes from our yearning for both kinds of completion. Along Psyche's path, we explore both aspects of our quest for love: How personal love can contribute to our spiritual unfoldment. And how Divine Love, in all its metaphysical glory, can help us grow toward psychological and emotional maturity.

part I

psyche's
four tasks

beginning the journey

Psyche's condition as she lay on the ground weeping with shame and grief at the pain she had caused herself and her divine husband mirrors the state of mind that brings many of us to the threshold of spiritual and personal growth. Often a life crisis or a sense of overwhelming unhappiness precipitates our first visit to a therapist's office, or spurs us to sign up for a transpersonal growth seminar or a meditation retreat. The Buddha taught that dissatisfaction with one's life is the first step on the spiritual journey. Suffering, he said, is the First Noble Truth; it motivates us to seek the path that leads to suffering's end. A wise old-timer in AA once told me, "Never remove an alcoholic's pain! The pain is what will save him." Whether our particular form of suffering is the end of an intimate relationship, the loss of a career, the death of a loved one, a serious illness, or some other serious setback, personal pain can provide the energy we need to move to the next stage of our evolution.

Psyche's first impulse after losing Eros was to throw herself into the river to drown her sorrows and end her life. The urge toward suicide, understood properly, often signals the need for some part of ourselves to die so that new consciousness can be born. I know this place well, as this is exactly how I felt lying on my bed, my third marriage in ruins, immediately before I was guided to find my true path in the pages of a book. For months I had been writing in my journal that I was sick to death of relationship melodramas and unwilling to go on creating such messes. A new way opened for me that day, born out of a sense of hopeless sorrow.

Painful endings are always a kind of death. But we have to allow ourselves to experience them fully in order for the way out to open from within. Too often, our attempts to drown our sorrows are less radical than suicide but more insidious. Addictions of all varieties, for instance, are a kind of death, a loss of self-will and rational judgment that is an instinctive response to pain we cannot manage. But addictions only mask our pain. They distract us into denying what's really wrong and lure us off course, sometimes for years.

In Psyche's case, her preconscious, superficial merging with Eros in the romantic night world of their marriage bed had to die in order for a mature love to be born. The immature Psyche knew her husband only through her physical senses—smell, taste, the sound of his voice, his touch. What was missing was sight—both outward seeing and self-knowledge or "in-sight." Because she could not see Eros,

Psyche did not know him in her rational, thinking mind. Reacting purely on physical sensation, without judgment, discrimination, or will—much as we all do when we are young—Psyche submitted in a dreamlike trance to whatever pleasurable sensations were offered her, from the unseen hands that bathed, fed, and clothed her, to the unseen choir that serenaded her, to her unseen husband who caressed her. Ironically, the very moment Psyche lit the lamp of consciousness and looked upon her husband, she lost him and so began the long and difficult journey toward the personal and spiritual awakening necessary to come to him again.

Failing in her attempt to kill herself—the river, fearful of Eros' divine power, refused to drown Psyche and instead carried her to the other shore—Psyche began her desperate wanderings. Her first encounter was with the goat-footed god Pan, who was sitting on the bank of the river playing his reed pipe, the nymph Echo on his lap. Pan, from whose name we get the word *panic*, is an ambivalent figure. On one hand, he represents wild, out-of-control energy. When we experience mad fits of rage, unrestrained weeping, or uncontrolled fear, we might say we have been seized by Pan. Such is often our first reaction to any loss or grief—an energetic response that is primitive, wrenching, body centered, irrational.

Yet Pan's energy, used correctly, can also fuel our evolutionary journey. As the god of nature and the countryside, Pan symbolizes natural sexual energy and a surefooted grounding in the physical world. He is the perfect mentor for Psyche, because the first task on her journey of initiation is to embrace fully her physical life here on earth. His words of comfort to the forlorn Psyche were prescient: "I see by your tearstained cheeks and wan expression that you are suffering the pangs of love," Pan told her. "Put aside your sorrow and appeal to Eros, the great god of love himself. Offer him your adoration and obedience, and he may relieve your pain." These words might seem at first to be a cruel irony. If Psyche *had* adored and obeyed Eros, she would not be in her current fix! Yet, at a deeper level, Pan was giving Psyche profound instruction. In her marriage to Eros, Psyche had been trapped in a state of childlike innocence. Pan was challenging her to awaken to adult womanhood and to use her natural human feminine wiles to win back Eros' love. He was giving her a reason to live and a goal to move toward as she began the perilous initiatory journey into maturity.

The details of Psyche's encounter with Pan underscore this message. When Psyche encountered him, Pan was teaching the nymph Echo to play the pipe, symbolically giving her a voice of her own, rather than one that only echoed others. This gives us a clue that Pan was also attempting to help Psyche find her voice, her true means of expression in the world. In pointing her toward Eros—erotic love—as the way out of her grief, Pan was telling her that mature love, though it may seem to threaten the self with dissolution, can be a path toward the self's fullest expression. Paradoxically, through selfless passion for another, Psyche would find her true self.

Poor Psyche could only shake her head, not comprehending the wisdom of Pan's words. In her panic, she did not

understand that the only cure for our soul's suffering is appealing to the very thing that hurt us. Running away from
our pain never ends it. Only when we find the courage to be
curious about our painful experiences, to examine them consciously and enter them deeply to decode their hidden messages, can we begin to heal. At the beginning of her
evolutionary journey, Psyche was not capable of such introspection, and so, with a courteous bow but without thanking
Pan for his advice, Psyche continued on her way.

The path of individuation is always fraught with paradox—
love and death, light and shadow. The depth psychology of
Carl Jung makes this clear. To be whole, Jung told us, we
have to come to know both the shadowy and the luminous
aspects of the god—and of ourselves. As I have mentioned,
the role of the shadow in the Psyche myth is enacted by
Psyche's two sisters. They symbolize the base parts of
the self, the parts we would just as soon ignore or deny—
jealousy, lust, envy, treachery, greed. Yet these shadowy parts
of the self can, paradoxically, trigger our journey into self-
knowledge. Paradox will always be present in any archetypal
process, especially at its beginning. We will encounter circumstances or be given advice that contains as much shadow
as light, depending on the way we view it. Our sacred task
is to struggle, with caution and discrimination, to comprehend both the dark and the light aspects of whatever we
encounter.

At the beginning of her journey to awakening, then, Psyche must confront the shadowy parts she has been denying,
and in so doing, move beyond them. After leaving Pan, Psy-

che journeyed to a town ruled by the husband of one of her two sisters. Making her way to the palace, Psyche told her sister what the lamp had revealed when she followed her sisters' advice. "When he discovered that I had betrayed him," Psyche told her sister, "the celestial god Eros who was my husband banished me from his bed. 'Begone,' he told me sternly, 'and I will marry your sister instead.' "

Hearing this, and overcome by lust and greed, Psyche's sister left her husband and ran to the crag from which the West Wind had once before wafted her down to visit Psyche's enchanted marriage palace. But this time, when she hurled herself from the cliff, the sister tumbled from rock to rock all the way down to a bloody death. Then Psyche made her way to the town where her other sister lived and told her the same cunning story, with the same bloody result.

These tricks by the innocent sweet-natured Psyche shock us greatly. But in allowing her shadow aspects to play out fully their baser natures, at a deeper level, Psyche was purging herself of those traits that the sisters symbolized. When we think about it carefully, we can also see that this episode echoes the advice Psyche had heard from Pan. In essence, Pan had counseled Psyche to throw herself at Eros' feet—but not as a suppliant. The wily Pan was advising Psyche not to shrink from using the stratagems of mature femininity to pursue and win back her man. In her childish innocence, Psyche had known nothing of such tricks. The ruse by which she took revenge on her sisters is her first test of the power of feminine wiles. By using subterfuge to destroy those forces that had sought to destroy her, Psyche began her entry into the adult world in which the simple certitudes of childhood are replaced by the complexities of shadow and light. By venturing into the shadow herself, Psyche signaled that her journey of individuation had truly begun.

While Psyche was beginning her struggles toward maturity on earth, Eros was caught in a similar drama in the heavenly realms. Still suffering the effects of the wound he received from Psyche's lamp, Eros had been imprisoned by his mother, Aphrodite, who was enraged at her son's disobedience and overflowing with resentment at Psyche. Languishing under his mother's spell, Eros symbolizes the *puer aeternus*, the eternal youth. We have all known such men, little boys of forty-five who have never grown up and who are not, consequently, capable of a mature relationship with a woman. Such men are what psychologists call female dependent. Like Eros, they fly around in the world of their own imaginations, whether through sports, lofty metaphysical philosophy, unrealistic artistic pursuits, or in the playgrounds of cyberspace. Cut off from the physicality of the material world, believing themselves to be superior to it, such men are also cut off from the earthy side of the masculine spirit. Their dependence on a mother figure interferes with their ability to give a mature woman what she needs and keeps them out of touch with the full expression of virile masculinity that could impel them toward real partnership.

This unhealthy mother-son dynamic also traps Aphrodite. Here the goddess of love and beauty plays out the archetypal role of the devouring mother. Such mothers are driven by their own unhealed wounds to hate and fear other women as rivals who might steal their sons' affection. Their goal is to keep their sons tied securely to the apron strings of immaturity and their hearts locked away for themselves.

Like Psyche, then, Eros has learning to do. To be worthy of reunion with her, he must evolve from an unconscious boy satisfied with secret couplings in the dark behind his mother's back to a mature man, capable of loving a woman in the bright light of full consciousness, a grown son capable of standing up to a devouring mother.

After dealing with her sisters, Psyche's next impulse was to ask for help from whatever wise being she could find. Seeing a temple on a nearby hill and hoping to find her husband there, Psyche hastened toward it. The shrine she entered belonged to Demeter, or Ceres, goddess of the harvest and of the earth's fruitfulness. Throwing herself at the feet of the goddess, Psyche begged for refuge and assistance, but Demeter refused her, saying, "I wish I could assist you, but my loyalty to my kinswoman Aphrodite forbids it. Leave my temple at once, but know that it is in your best interest that I refuse you my protection." Even more cast down and dejected, Psyche wandered on to a temple in a valley, this one sacred to Hera, queen of heaven and goddess of marriage. But like Demeter, Hera had been warned by Aphrodite of Psyche's plight. Knowing of Aphrodite's displeasure with the girl, Hera, too, turned her face away, saying, "I am forbidden by high law to harbor someone else's runaway slave. Your case is with Aphrodite, so to her temple you must go to face your mistress directly."

beginning the journey

Our own spiritual journey often begins with just such desperate appeals. Our first reaction to suffering is often the belief that our salvation lies in some greater being—a spiritual teacher, a therapist, a new lover—whom we invest with godlike abilities and expect to rescue us from our problems. When I met my first spiritual teacher, I elevated him in my mind to superhuman status and responded in a nearly childlike way to his teachings, without rational judgment or discernment, hoping my life would be magically fulfilled by my relationship with him.

If the person in whom we place our hopes for salvation is spiritually mature and psychologically grounded, he or she will refuse to entertain our inappropriate expectations. Luckily, the goddesses to whom Psyche appealed did not allow her to hook on. Some of us are not so lucky and spend years in fruitless bondage to the belief that someone or something outside ourselves can save us.

Thrown back on her own resources, which is the place where all true learning begins, Psyche made a desperate decision. Fearing that the choice meant certain death and yet seeing no other option, she resolved "to borrow a little male courage," as Apuleius puts it, and seek out Aphrodite directly to beg the divine mother of Eros to forgive her and to help her win back her husband. Under Aphrodite's stern direction, Psyche began her labors, four tasks that mark her transformation from preconscious immaturity to personal and spiritual adulthood.

As we will discover, these tasks are ours as well. In the symbolic language of myth, they represent four stages in the process of individuation—steps on our journey toward manifesting the Divine Self we were born to become. Each task gives us the opportunity to embody one of the four elements, symbolic of the four levels of consciousness that make up a mature human being. In the first task, we embody earth and gain consciousness of the physical domain. In the second, we embody water and enter mature emotional consciousness. The third teaches us about air, symbol of the mental realm, while the fourth and final task takes us to the realm of fire, where we enter into mature spirituality.

Psyche's four tasks will also open us to an understanding of the inner dynamics of depth psychology. The first three tasks teach Psyche to reclaim various aspects of her inner masculine, qualities she had denied and projected onto Eros, such as discernment, assertiveness, prudence, direction, and focused intention. The fourth task gives Psyche the opportunity to descend to her unconscious depths and experience the gift of feminine surrender in order that she might reclaim her mature and queenly feminine qualities. Only when Psyche has brought the masculine and feminine parts of her inner nature into balance can she fulfill her destiny and become the human goddess of personal love, a worthy partner for her divine husband. Read in this way, Psyche's journey is a study of the potentially transformative energy of a love relationship. The male and female fuse, then separate, then fuse again until both are purified sufficiently to consummate a true union.

As you study each task, you will begin to see how each lesson pertains to you. Reading through that lens, you'll see that these are your initiatory labors of love, tasks that will purify you and lead you to your Source.

Sorting the Seeds

When the terrified Psyche first came into the presence of Aphrodite, the goddess berated her. "So, you deign to come to me," the goddess stormed, "while your husband, my foolish son, lies moaning and gravely wounded on my golden bed. Now you shall know the fury of the goddess whose rightful worship you usurped." With that, Aphrodite fell upon Psyche, pulling her hair, scratching her face, and tearing her clothes.

"I myself will make trial of your worth, you terrible girl," Aphrodite raged and called for her servants to bring great quantities of seeds—wheat, poppy, barley, millet, lentils, peas, and beans—and mix them together in a huge heap. "Do you see this pile of seeds?" Aphrodite demanded. "Prove to me how quick fingered you are by sorting them into their different kinds. Put each seed in its proper place by this evening when I return, or death will be the consequence."

Though she sounds here just like the wicked stepmothers of fairy tales, Aphrodite is also speaking with the voice of destiny. The passive Psyche needs a strong push to become heroic. The seeds Aphrodite asks Psyche to sort are the seeds of her transformation. The underlying message of the task is that the seeds of evolutionary growth lie dormant in our psyches from before we were born, just waiting for us to get busy and sort them out.

Poor Psyche had no idea how to begin. She just sat there, paralyzed, stupefied, silent. Like Eve in the Garden for whom everything had been provided, Psyche had been largely a passive participant in her own life story. Unconscious and unaware, she accepted without judgment whatever happened to her. At this point in her journey, she didn't even know that she was a self, a being who could reason, make choices, and take action.

Jungian depth psychology, one of the most vital and profound spiritual psychologies the world has known, views the unconscious mind as a spectrum. At one end of the spectrum are sensation and instinct, those habitual actions and reactions that, in the well-balanced psyche, create order and stability. We begin life at the instinctive end of the spectrum. Newborns are merged with their mothers so profoundly that they cannot tell where their bodies end and their mothers' begin. Depth psychologists call this state *participation mystique*, which I described earlier as that primitive condition in which one cannot clearly distinguish between oneself and an object or a concept to which one is relating, which is therefore imbued with a kind of magical significance or power. The childhood stage that we call the terrible twos marks an important step in the process of individuation. By saying "No!" and disobeying, a child learns that she is separate from her mother. When this initial differentiation is encouraged by healthy parenting, the child begins to claim her own interests and to see herself as an individual who can make choices.

But even in adulthood, we sometimes function primarily from the instinctive end of the spectrum. In the unevolved manifestation of this state, we are creatures of habit, driven by sensuous urges, traveling through life on automatic pilot. The restraining power of judgment is weak, and we lack the will to discriminate between helpful and hurtful actions. As a consequence, we fall easily into the traps of compulsive behavior, anxious fantasy, or obsessive doubt, often having no idea how we got ourselves into such a mess.

Addictions are one way this pattern manifests, but there are less serious ways we experience it. For instance, say you are working on a project and become obsessed with making it perfect. Instead of moving forward with calm and steady progress, you lapse into feverish, robotic activity, staying up all night, forgetting to eat, becoming so enmeshed in detail that you lose sight of the overall purpose of the work.

At the other end of Jung's spectrum are our spiritual impulses, those higher cognitions that put us in touch with the sacred and imbue us with revelations of the deep meaning of people and experiences. In this part of consciousness reside the archetypes—those universal patterns and images that shine through everyday events and illuminate them with spiritual significance. When we function at this end of the spectrum in a healthy way, we are flooded with emotional responses that teach us the sacred meaning of things around us. I know of nothing that heals a wounded psyche more rapidly than a genuine mystical experience—a feeling that one has been touched by a god! A person whose sense of self is strong can contain the energy of such revelations and view them as enriching and life-expanding insights without being overwhelmed by their power.

When our sense of self is weak, however, mystical experiences can be risky. The danger is losing ourselves in the mists of unreality, creating a false spirituality in which ordinary, grounded perceptions are suspended. When we first embark on spiritual practice, our ardor sometimes feels like falling in love with the Divine. The psyche may be flooded with extraordinary experiences for which we have no context or understanding. This state can be dangerous, as our powerful emotional responses to the numinous can short-circuit our rational judgment and make us vulnerable to abuse or exploitation. In this condition, we may overidentify with some larger-than-life ideal, be it person or cause, and lose ourselves in an overwhelming flood of spiritual or emotional fervor. The tragedy that befell followers of David Koresh in Waco, Texas, and the mass suicide cult triggered by the appearance of the Hale-Bopp comet illustrate the contemporary dangers of this pattern.

As she faced her first labor, Psyche vacillated between these two unevolved extremes of response. In her early marriage, as we have seen, Psyche was living in a fool's paradise, driven purely by sensuous/instinctive urges. Without the guidance of her thinking function, Psyche was "in the dark" about her husband and about herself. There was no part of her that could separate and evaluate what was happening to her, no consciousness able to be self-reflective. As in the participation mystique of an infant, Psyche had merged with Eros through touch and sensation rather than through choice and will. It is no wonder that she was so easily swayed by her sisters' jealous schemes, as she had neither reason nor its mirror function, intuition, to judge her sisters' motives or intuit the falseness of their projected fantasies.

At the spiritual end of the spectrum, Psyche was in similarly dangerous waters. In her girlhood, she had accepted the homage of her father's subjects, who hailed her as the new Aphrodite and worshipped her with rites that belonged to the goddess. Alienated from her human identity, Psyche believed that she was Beauty itself, rather than a beautiful but human girl. In Jungian terms, we might say that she was overidentified with her larger-than-life "mother," Aphrodite, her self-identity lost in the archetype with whom she was linked.

The first step on the path toward soul maturity is developing the conscious awareness to avoid the pitfalls of these two extremes of response. The healthy psyche is able to use the stabilizing routines of the instinctive function to differentiate instantly between helpful and dangerous situations and so assure our physical safety. Think of how difficult it would be to drive a car without instincts, and you'll understand what I mean. At the spiritual end of the spectrum, the challenge is approaching the sacred with a strong sense of personal identity, maintaining the rational grounding that allows us to check out for ourselves the truth of what we encounter. A mature spirituality requires not blind faith but intelligent faith—a willingness to question and evaluate the worth and meaning of spiritual experiences and the teachings of any spiritual guide.

Soul growth requires, further, that we become familiar with the entire spectrum of the unconscious, both the animal-like instincts and the spiritual and archetypal dimensions, so that we can gain access to each when appropriate. Instincts tempered by conscious awareness give us the ability to sort things according to their function. Once we can see the people, objects, and activities in our lives clearly, know them as separate from ourselves, and define their purpose, spirit can "play" with them, breathing into them feeling, symbolic meaning, and spiritual significance.

The soul skill I am describing here, so essential to making wise choices about the things in our life, is discernment. We use discernment to separate out those people, objects, and activities that are helpful to our growth from those that are a waste of time, or what's worse, harmful or addictive. Discernment helps us at either extreme of the unconscious spectrum. When discernment is married to our instinctive responses, we can apply will and reason to combat addictive and compulsive behaviors. When we apply discernment to our spiritual responses, we avoid losing ourselves in powerful floods of spiritual feeling.

What does Psyche's story teach us about how to develop discernment? First, it tells us that in order to be discerning, we have to get in touch with our instincts and put them to work in a grounded way. In the symbolic language of myth, as is the case in dreams, each character, object, or event represents an aspect of the central character. As she faces the first task, Psyche's developing powers of discernment are represented by an army of industrious ants. As the abject Psyche contemplates the heap of seeds before her, the helpful ants appear and quickly and efficiently sort the seeds into their various kinds.

The close-to-ground but purposeful activity of ants makes them a perfect symbol for the instinctive ability to create order in our lives. Ants are doers. In the symbolic language of myth, ants are considered children of the earth. They tackle a task directly, with ingenuity and a strong sense of purpose. They are not easily dissuaded by the size or complexity of a problem; they start at the beginning, doing first things first and persisting until the job is done. Our antlike qualities are those that help us accomplish the heap of tasks we face each day, starting with the most immediate or the nearest and working quickly and efficiently until everything is finished. Ants don't waste time contemplating the implications of every step or looking at the big picture. They divide a huge project into manageable chunks and then simply get going.

The instinctual forces that can transform chaos into order are already present in Psyche, just as they are in each of us. The task of sorting the seeds gives Psyche the opportunity to put these dormant qualities to work. Our own lives give us many opportunities to practice the same skills. Reorganizing your life to accommodate a new baby or a new job, a spouse's retirement or some other major life change, challenges us to sort the seeds of our lives, just as Psyche did. This task seems to be necessary to our growth—so much so, that if circumstances do not provide an opportunity for us to engage in it, we often create the chance for ourselves. Perhaps this explains why, when everything seems to be going well, we sometimes "tear up our playhouse" and create chaos in our lives that must be ordered in some new way. The tip-off that this is going on is when we catch ourselves doing or saying things that break down existing structures or relationships as though something beyond us has control. When this occurs, you might surmise that the archetype of transformation has been activated in your life, and your soul is shaking things up in order to move you toward some new adventure in consciousness.

As a function of the thinking or rational mind, discernment is linked more with masculine-style than with feminine-style thinking. Remember, masculine and feminine as I am using them are not necessarily linked to gender. As I have explained, both men and women have inner masculine and feminine qualities and do, of course, think in both styles. Masculine-style thinking is oriented toward outer objects. It analyzes and separates, diagnoses and labels. Linked to logic and the thinking function, masculine-style thought brings order out of chaos and directs the will toward the achievement of desired goals. Feminine-style thinking is oriented toward wholes rather than toward parts. It is not designed to isolate and define various aspects of reality but rather to intuit or grasp the overall meaning and significance of a thing or experience. Many of us are never taught that we all have a contrasexual opposite living inside us that must develop if we are to be whole. The process of individuation requires that we master both sides of our nature, as each brings us important skills. To function at an optimal level, men and women need both masculine and feminine styles of thinking and the awareness to determine when each style is most appropriate.

Psyche's plight when faced with the heap of seeds, however, is especially poignant for women. The practical concerns of modern life ask women to use masculine-style thinking to get organized, set priorities, make choices, create order out of chaos. The conflicting demands on women's time, juggling career, parenting, household, and relationship tasks, while making time for personal and spiritual growth, are no less difficult than Psyche's challenge of sorting the seeds. Women especially need to learn to sort creatively in order to make healthy choices for themselves and their families. Millet is not the same as wheat. Beans and poppy seeds have different qualities and different functions. Sorting the seeds is an apt metaphor for the choices women make each day.

Thus in accomplishing the first task Aphrodite set for her, Psyche learns several critical lessons:

- She discovers the importance of being an active participant in the process of living rather than passively waiting for events to happen.
- She learns that danger lies at either extreme of consciousness—that instincts must be tempered by awareness, and spirituality grounded in a strong sense of self-identity.
- She experiences the complexity of her twinned nature and

learns that to be whole, she must develop both masculine and feminine styles of thinking.

- Finally, she learns that discernment can help create order out of chaos and direct the will toward the achievement of desired goals.

What can we learn from Psyche's first task? Perhaps our most important lesson is that when we are centered in our true being, aspects of our consciousness we didn't even know we had will provide the help we need. For, like Psyche, our nature is twinned. Not only do our psyches have both masculine and feminine components but we are also simultaneously human and divine. As we come to recognize these essential dualities, we discover to our delight that our human/Divine Self is greater than any condition that might arise and that we can accomplish any task, no matter how impossible it might seem! We discover as well that our growth into personal and spiritual maturity requires a strong sense of personal identity, for how we define ourselves influences strongly the quality of our life.

The ancient Hindu teachings regarding the chakras offer a useful parallel here. The chakras, as you may know, are a series of seven energy centers aligned vertically along the center line of the human body, from the base of the spine to the crown of the head. The chakras bridge our soul body with our physical body. Seen metaphorically, each is an archetype for a stage in our personal and spiritual development. As we master the tasks associated with each chakra, we ascend from purely physical consciousness to a refined spiritual sensibility. Each chakra is a stepping-stone on our journey toward actualizing the human/Divine Self we were born to become.

The task of the first chakra, located at the base of the spine, is grounding ourselves in the basic will to live as an individual self, with a clear sense of personal identity. We must fully incarnate here. This foundation supports all future growth. Before she can realize her dual nature as human and divine, Psyche must incarnate fully as a human girl and master the skills necessary to survive in a human body. Among the most important of these, as we have seen, are the physical instincts that keep her safe. The ants remind Psyche of this important stage of development and model for her a grounded and purposeful approach to problem solving.

Though the journey Psyche has begun toward personal and spiritual maturity will be long and arduous, and her self-confidence will often flag, the stable grounding she achieves by accomplishing this first task will keep her on course. Her original union with her divine husband and partner was a physical, body-centered experience. As she differentiates herself from her larger-than-life "mother," this original connection, grounded in the body, will hold her passionately in its grip and keep her striving steadily toward her goal. Time and again, she may doubt her ability to endure the sacrifices her passion will require and wonder whether she and Eros will ever reunite. But these internal doubts and struggles will, by friction, keep a fire burning in Psyche's being to propel her forward on her path.

We, too, have a goal to strive toward. For like Psyche, we

came from an undifferentiated state of divine oneness into incarnation in human form. Like her, we must establish a stable grounding in the physical as the basis for our journey toward higher consciousness. Whether this means working to free ourselves from addictions to food, cigarettes, alcohol, or drugs; or whether it requires that we "sort our seeds" and put our house, our professional life, or our relationships in order, the task of the first chakra is to sort out the physical aspects of our life as a preliminary to further growth.

As spiritual beings in human form, we ascend and descend in consciousness on the way to becoming a fully blossomed self. Well grounded in the physical, it is safe for us to re-member and revisit the divine unity from which we came, because we are no longer at risk of losing ourselves in the mists of spiritual consciousness. After completing this first task, we can safely play in the higher worlds of spiritual reality, since we are anchored to reality by a well-defined sense of personal identity.

The following exercise in self-reflection will give you the opportunity to practice some of the skills necessary for grounding yourself in the physical and to apply them to sort-ing the heap of seeds you face in your life.

Self-reflection

Creating Order in Our Physical Lives

One of the main challenges in shifting from unconscious to conscious living is learning to sort essentials from nonessentials. Essentials keep us moving toward our personal and spiritual goals. Nonessentials distract us. Before proceeding on our sacred journey, we must claim our earth element by creating order in our physical lives.

This exercise in self-reflection can help you bring to awareness aspects of your life that may be blocking your growth. It trains you in decisiveness and rational discernment, two traits we must develop in the early stages of our soul's journey. We have to decide before anything actually moves. Then we can apply judgment and discrimination to pursuing those goals our consciousness deems essential.

Find a quiet place to sit in reflection for a while with a notebook and pen. Take a blank sheet of paper and divide it vertically into three columns.

Now, in your mind's eye, take yourself through a typical week of your life. In the first column, write down the ways you spend your time and the approximate amount of time you spend on each activity. Note also whether each activity is done with intention or unconsciously. For instance, you may write that you spend two hours a day watching television. Then ask yourself how much of that time was spent idly switching channels and how much was watching programs you consciously selected to view.

In the second column, list those activities from your first column that you consider to be essential to your life's work and purpose—those things that help keep you on your path. Be dead honest with yourself and take as much time as you need to reflect about this question.

In column three, list the nonessentials from column one.

Then reflect on each, noting which you choose to keep in your life and which you are willing to drop.

Now take some time to think about your life goals as seen through the ways you are spending your time. Ask yourself:

- What am I here for?
- Am I willing to live in my body, or do I excessively seek out-of-body experiences?
- Do the ways I spend my time advance my goals or block them?
- In what ways do I cut myself off from the possibilities that life affords me?
- What passions emanating from deep within me do I follow?
- How might I learn to distinguish between drives that arise from my soul's connection to Source and those that serve only my ego?

Reflect also on the ways in which you, like Psyche, have allowed confusion to keep you from moving forward. Spontaneously let flow from your pen reflections on how indecision or lack of discernment manifests in your life. For instance, do you:

- leave your body so that you remain unfocused?
- seek ways to avoid your true tasks by scurrying here and there, thinking up ways to distract yourself?
- put your mind in neutral and refuse to think?

- tell yourself you are too overwhelmed and deserve a break?
- lie to yourself about how hard you work?
- use "cycles" and "rhythms" as your excuse for not moving forward?
- belittle physical reality as being less important than the mental or spiritual realm?

We often resort to confusion when we don't want to deal with what's trying to emerge from the uncomfortable unknown that lurks below the surface of our waking life. Confusion is a way to hide, a cover we use to keep from knowing what's coming next. It is a form of spiritual laziness that keeps us from focusing on our intentions. Halfway measures will never do on the soul's journey. No matter how confused and undecided we feel, we must be heroic in our willingness and courage. And because we have come here to make the incarnational journey, we must learn to plant our feet purposefully right here on earth.

To overcome our unwillingness to sort the seeds and set our lives on track, we must strive with all our rational might to give shape to our deepest yearnings, hopes, wishes, fears, and fantasies. Once we are willing to focus our intuition and grounded will on what's really important, new abilities will arise to assist us. An industrious army of inner ants will mobilize to help us create order and progress toward our goals.

Psyche's first task taught her to forge ahead, no matter how impossible the task, to pursue her divine intention to reunite with Eros, the source of her inspiration. Following her example, we too can become whole and wholly blessed.

A Note about Daily Practice

Once we begin to awaken, our psyche's only desire is to become fully conscious. Keeping this process in motion, however, requires a daily commitment. A spiritual diary is a good way to stay focused on personal and spiritual goals.

A spiritual diary can be an excellent accompaniment to reading this book. Why not begin today by purchasing a small notebook, one that you can carry with you nearly all the time? Here you can jot down ideas, feelings, or revelations that you believe can further your awakening. You can write anything from an unedited ventilation of a strong emotional reaction, with comments to yourself about what caused you to react so strongly, to profound directives that you intuit as coming from your highest self. Be sure to date each entry. Begin this process each morning as you awaken, and end the process each evening before you go to bed.

Keeping a spiritual journal can help prevent you from getting caught up in fragmented and wasteful energies. It sets up a rapport between Universal Mind, your psyche, and your human will, a potent combination which can bring forth your own particular talents and genius. It highlights difficulties your psyche may be trapped in and suggests ways to release these blocks. A spiritual journal can help you hear the inner voice of the soul more strongly and move you into co-creative cooperation with the universe.

So begin today! Making a commitment to daily journaling strengthens your will and helps you discern the patterns and texture of the seeds that make up everyday life. As you process through this book, you will find other suggestions for using your spiritual journal.

TASK TWO

Gathering the Fleece

Seeing that Psyche had completed the task of sorting the seeds, Aphrodite again flew into a rage. To be outdone by this human girl was more than she could bear. "This feat was not accomplished by you, you dreadful wench," she stormed. "It was the work of my son who loves you so!" Now even more determined to revenge herself on the impertinent girl, the goddess set an even more impossible task for Psyche.

"We'll see what you're made of, you wretched creature. I have need of the shining golden fleece of the rams of the sun who graze near the river. I wish to weave it into a shawl to cover my shoulders at the Great Sea Festival being held in my honor. Gather the fleece and bring it to me. Do not dare return without it, or it will be the end of you!"

Poor Psyche, all beaten up and forlorn, was devastated once more. This time she was certain that she had no choice but to kill herself, and so she left quite peacefully, planning to throw herself off the cliff overhanging the river and so end her sorrowful life once and for all. But when she arrived at the cliff edge, she heard the murmuring of a large green reed growing near the bank of the river, its sweet music breathing a message she could hear clearly.

"Psyche," said the reed, "though you are wracked with woe, do not let this stop you from your task. You are not so powerless as you think. The rams you seek draw their fierce power from the light of the sun. If you approach them by day, they will surely batter you. But at dusk, when the sun's brilliance ebbs, their energies dissipate, and their wild frenzies cease. Hide in the bushes nearby until you see that the rams have been lulled by the soft breezes of evening. When their breathing is steady and they all lie perfectly still, you can gather the strands of golden fleece that cling to the trees of the grove in which they graze. So go now, Psyche. Keep harmony with the rhythms of the day, and be brave!"

Psyche listened carefully to these wise words and made no delay in doing what the reed suggested. That evening, when dusk had quieted the crazed rampages of the solar rams, she crept into the grove and gathered enough golden fleece to fulfill the demands of Aphrodite.

As we have noted, the characters and events of a myth or dream often stand for inner aspects of the central figure. Given this, how should we interpret the details of Psyche's second task? First, we should note that water, such as the river mentioned here, often signifies the emotions. Water has many moods, as do our emotions, from violent storms to glassy calm. Moreover, its surface appearance does not always reveal what is going on underneath. When faced with an emotional crisis, we even say that we are "in deep water" or "in over our heads."

If the river stands for Psyche's emotional nature, what does the reed represent? We note that the reed's roots lie deep in the watery world of the emotions, but its green top extends into the air. In contrast to water, air generally signifies the world of the mind, a realm of clarity, reason, and common sense. We often describe a new perspective on a problem, for instance, as "a breath of fresh air." Because it links the water and the air, the reed seems to be a means of bridging emotions and reason. Traditionally, the emotional realm is regarded as feminine, while the mental/intellectual realm is considered to be masculine. Thus the reed points toward Psyche's need to balance feminine and masculine, heart and head, as a central task of her journey into maturity.

Up to this point, Psyche's emotional life had been that of a little girl. The benighted love she felt for Eros, as we have noted, lacked the light of mature consciousness. Her desperate flights to seek help from the motherly goddesses were likewise the impulses of a frightened child. Each challenge or setback threw her anew into a suicidal panic. She simply could not *think* of anything she might do. In this second task, she is being given the opportunity to bring these girlish, out-of-control emotional responses into balance with the conscious drive and problem-solving power of the creative masculine principle. Psyche must learn that it is no longer sufficient for her to just be. She must also do—but she must act wisely and well.

In order to accomplish this task, Psyche must figure out a way to use her head and outsmart the rams. The rams whose golden power Psyche has been challenged to gather are a potent symbol of the most aggressive and dangerous aspects of masculine power. Many women fear that they will be annihilated if they come too close to this source of primal energy when it is embodied in a man. But Psyche is being asked to do more here. In order to grow toward mature consciousness, she must steal or take in some of this masculine power for herself, as a balance to her overly feminine tendencies.

Seen in this light, the rams represent two extremes of Psyche's nature, the docile and the crazed. Both are aspects of Psyche's shadow self. Because she lacked knowledge of her inner, subjective side, Psyche's emotional responses were often out of control—crazed, even. The rambunctious, overtly sexual energy of the rams terrified Psyche, as she was as yet unable to balance the opposites and use the power and potency of her inner masculine to energize her actions. At the other extreme, Psyche's overly passive responses were equally unevolved. From the time she allowed herself to be bound on the mountaintop to await her monster husband, through her meek acceptance of Eros' peculiar conditions for their marriage and her submissive acquiescence to her sisters' selfish and greedy demands, Psyche had been docile to the point of self-destruction. In fact, the only action she seemed willing to take was to kill herself! In learning to link her emotional life to her ability to reason, Psyche began to emerge from the shadow of unconscious emotionality into the clearer air of willed intention and controlled action.

Psyche's lesson here is ours as well. To bring clarity to our emotional nature, we must come to understand how the human shadow works to make us whole—or, perhaps a better way of saying it, how the shadow works *us*. Our shadow side lives in our emotional body. We often become aware of it when we overreact emotionally to some situation. Once we are aware of this tendency, we can train ourselves to read the signals of the emotions. When we catch ourselves reacting too strongly to something, we can stop and ask, "Which of my denied qualities am I confronting here? What aspect of my shadow side is being tweaked by this situation?" The human psyche contains both light and dark—conscious reactions and those whose motivation is shadowed or unconscious. Understanding this, we can use our emotions as a reliable compass to warn us that we are going off track and to help us steer back to a middle course. Creative self-observation is the key. When we are in the dark about our emotional responses, we can be overwhelmed by our emotional nature and believe that because we are feeling something strongly, it must be the truth. But we must always remember: we are not our emotions! Strong feelings are pointers to something that is in process within us, something in the throes of transformation that is coming up to die and be reborn in a new guise.

The strategy that the reed suggested—or rather, since the reed is symbolically an aspect of Psyche, that Psyche devised—is to wait patiently, watch carefully, and gather the fleece indirectly. Approaching the rams by day in a direct, forceful, and assertive masculine manner would prove fatal. Instead, Psyche needed to temper her will to action with feminine patience and intuition and find a way to accomplish the task without arousing the rams' fury. I call this skill standing at the nil point—a position of perfect balance, from which we banish all energies that can harm us. In overcoming her fear of the primitive power of the masculine as symbolized by the rams, while at the same time, controlling her excessive reactivity and impatience, Psyche became equal to the challenge the rams presented. As Psyche was discovering, in every polarity there is a moment when opposing extremes come into equilibrium, as with a pendulum. Standing at this nil point, Psyche experienced a healthy equality between the positive masculine qualities of assertiveness, focused intention, and action, and the positive feminine qualities of instinctive self-protection, intuition, and right timing. From this place of stability, she could begin to manifest her destiny.

At various times in our lives, we all become lopsided—either too masculine or too feminine in the way we approach things. When we are unstable in this dimension of our psyches, we often feel ourselves to be victims of our feelings, especially painful or fearful ones. I understand intimately what Psyche was going through during this phase of her awakening, as I have experienced in myself the unsettling effects of swinging too far to an extreme. Raised in Texas as a traditional southern belle, my process of growing up centered on overcoming a tendency to be too feminine. When

I'm depressed or in a weakened emotional state, I can still feel the urge to go all helpless and talk in a little-girl voice instead of my real one. Or I become seductive and manipulative, which also isn't the grown-up me.

As I now realize, this imbalance has been the crucible of experience that has challenged me to become whole. Over and over, circumstances have forced me to take on tasks that I thought some man would handle for me. Taking on our denied side is never easy, even once we've made the commitment to do so. When I first decided to develop my inner masculine and become more rational and objective, I frankly didn't know how to do it. So I overcompensated for being a southern belle by becoming a queen of swords, given to "striking" people too directly every time I spotted something that needed to be confronted. Being intuitive and a therapist to boot, I knew just how to aim at a person's Achilles' heel and could easily cut them to the bone with my sword of truth. Today, I am conscious of this tendency in myself. When I am off the mark, I can feel it, and I make an effort to come back into equilibrium.

When we fail to preserve proper balance between the opposing forces of our psyche, we risk an enantiodromia response. *Enantiodromia* is the Greek word for the psyche's way of turning us around to the opposite—toward whatever qualities we have been denying in ourselves. It comes into play whenever we are living out of one side of some emotional polarity. For instance, for a time I swung between being a cloyingly sweet southern belle and a confrontational queen of swords, with nothing in between. A television minister who preaches passionately against the sins of the flesh and then is arrested with a prostitute is another example. So is a couple whose Christmas letter celebrates their perfect family life, yet within months find themselves embroiled in a nasty divorce. When the shadow side in any relationship is denied—like the minister denying the human need for an exciting sex life or the couple covering up the problems in their marriage, even to themselves—the anger, hurt, deception, and fear that has been repressed builds up steam in the subconscious until it explodes, pouring out all the negativity for everyone to see.

Developing a sound and balanced feeling nature is difficult. We must strive to live from both sides of our emotional continuum as much as possible—masculine and feminine, light and shadow, outer and inner—and never become too extreme on either side of any polarity. When we err to one side or the other, we should be aware that enantiodromia is just around the corner, biding its time to swing us to the denied side and embarrass us greatly. The humiliation can be our first step in owning a grave and thoughtless imbalance. The human psyche is not the least bit interested in perfection. It wants to be centered and complete, to know both sides of everything in life all the way through.

So where do you fall in this dynamic? Stop for a minute and examine the tendencies of your emotional nature. Are you so soft and heartfelt, so expanded and vague, that you can't seem to cope with interpersonal problems without excessive emotionality? Or are you so hard and analytical that you run roughshod over people's feelings, while being afraid to reveal how you really feel? How would you name the opposing tendencies of your emotional body? What undeveloped emotional qualities need to grow up for you to come into balance? These are excellent questions for you to explore the next time you write in your spiritual journal.

You might also think about the role timing plays in your emotional life. If you are like me, you can probably recall times when you've erred at a crucial point of interaction by blurting out the truth at the wrong time, saying too much too quickly, or when the other is ill prepared to hear it. Or perhaps you've noticed how sometimes your emotions have simply gotten the best of you, and you have said or done something that ended a relationship, when truly, only a disagreement or misunderstanding was taking place. Sometimes we act too quickly and say or do things that cannot be undone. When complications arise in our dealings with others, we are often best served by moving inside to stand at nil, acting only when we have come to silence at that place of inner balance.

The same is true in the dynamics of group interaction. In the psychospiritual group work we do at Eupsychia events, we've found that at around four every afternoon, the "dragon" energy gets very strong and starts to create havoc. At that time of day cigarette smokers can hardly sit still and those accustomed to a happy hour start to need a drink. Intellectuals in the room also get "hungry" and demand that the teacher give them immediate answers to complicated questions or irritably throw out ill-timed comments that lead nowhere.

We've learned to treat this phenomenon with humor and meet the dragon lightheartedly when he uncoils in every corner of the room. We schedule a break every afternoon at four so that we can "feed the hungry dragon." By doing so, we honor the natural rhythms of the day rather than being so arrogant as to believe that we can simply ignore them and overcome their disruptive power. When we take responsibility for aligning our personal wills with the greater and higher Will, we can find the right approach to almost any situation. We can learn to not fear our dragon nature but to tame the dragon with the female wiles of lighthearted compassion.

There is, of course, another way to balance the masculine and the feminine and that is to come into relationship with our opposite. The gender myths of many traditions hold that the masculine and feminine principles were once united. The origin of mature sexuality is the drive to reunite these separated contraries. In fact, I would go so far as to say that love is the intense yearning to join together with what we ourselves are missing. The sexes *are* different—complementary opposites, to be sure. The point of love is not to blend two people into one spiceless, diluted soup. Rather, mature love asks men and women to appreciate each other's qualities, assimilate those that each needs to become whole, and express this richness of response with appropriateness and right timing. When we try to merge the masculine and feminine too soon—such as by marrying too young—we achieve, at best, a premature transcendence. Such couplings seldom last, for they are not a conscious and mature consummation of our need for completion.

Chinese philosophy names the opposing qualities of this duality yin and yang. Chinese teachings about wholeness—physical, emotional, mental, and spiritual—have always been based on the wisdom of balancing these opposites. Until we find the balance between yin and yang within ourselves, we often try to achieve it by coupling with a person who represents the contrasexual "other" for us. This is how we practice, and it's why opposites attract. However, when our own development is immature, we often fall into relationships of needy love in which we try to get from the other person qualities that we cannot find in ourselves. We saw this dynamic at work in Psyche's young love for Eros. Since she had no masculine force operating through her, Psyche projected her masculine side onto Eros, who did all the thinking and made all the decisions for her. Many typical relationship dysfunctions stem from such imbalances within the individuals who make up the pair. In some couples, both members are too yin and passive; in others, both are too yang and controlling.

When each individual in a couple is balanced along the masculine and feminine polarity, two whole people are relating to each other. This is the highest form of human love. In mature relationships, when the feminine is speaking with its appropriate voice, the masculine principle stands behind it and supports its expression with the validating word: "Yes, she has the right to feel that. Research backs her up." In this case, the masculine is acting as a protector or redeeming god. And when the masculine needs to come forth, the feminine principle stands behind it and supports its expression with love, acceptance, and encouragement: "Of course, you'll give a wonderful presentation. You know your subject, and you are the best." Here the feminine is acting as a nurturer, a goddess of the earth.

At some point, wholeness demands that we "marry" that from which we can never be separated, bringing together masculine and feminine, conscious and unconscious, seen and unseen, our divine and human natures. To put it plainly, our outward behavior strives to match our inner feelings and attitudes until there is no discrepancy.

Looked at through the lens of the chakra system, the task of gathering the fleece deals with the energies of the second chakra. The second chakra, located at the body's power center below the navel, is the symbolic nexus of our sex drive and the point at which our passions are balanced with our emotional/relational nature. To gather the fleece, Psyche had to control her feminine fear of the rams' virile masculinity. Moreover, she could not act rashly or behave unconsciously, especially in her sense of timing. All of her passions had to be contained or she might die. When we heal the energies of our second chakra, we're capable of positive enjoyment of our instinctive impulses and free to delight in the pleasures of sexuality. At the same time, we are capable of controlling our emotional drives and refraining from using our sexual or passionate energies when they are inappropriate.

Two types of people have an especially hard time accessing the generative and creative energies of the second chakra.

One is the soft, overly feminine person who is afraid to reveal his or her real strengths and talents. Such people hold back passively, fearing a reprimand or their own success, hoping that some miracle will happen that will bring them their true expression in life. They lack the assertiveness and directness necessary to make creative manifestation possible. Creativity is also a challenge to those men and women who have a powerful need to control. This type is not able to stand the fact that creativity requires chaos. They want to order things analytically before the processes of creation have even taken hold. Consequently their creativity is blocked.

In both cases, the solution requires that we honor the needs of the feminine and masculine parts of ourselves—the emotional heart as well as the thinking head. Purifying the heart, where the feeling nature resides, removes our feminine fear of the powerful, generative energies of creativity. Once we accept emotionally that transformation always requires us to reveal ourselves through some kind of direct and forceful self-expression, we won't be so afraid to come out of hiding and to allow our feelings to be stirred up so that new creation can come through. But the head also must let go of its masculine need for control. We must recognize that either/or thinking rarely works. We must keep our thoughts clear of any illusions about life being orderly and neat and allow the messy process of creativity to unfold with all its ambiguities—its chaotic discomforts and its passionate joys.

Before we follow Psyche into the next task of her journey, let's stop and reflect on how this second task relates to us.

Making Right Use of Emotional/Creative Force

How accepting are you of the messy creative processes of your life—the relationships or circumstances that surround you, whether they are painful or pleasurable? Is there a person, or some part of your life, that you wish would just go away so that you wouldn't have to deal with it? If so, name it to yourself right now.

Anything that is really bothering you, that you want to push away, is probably crying out for your attention. Strong aversion can be a signal that you are not taking responsibility for some aspect of your life. It clues you in that something is going on unconsciously that might jump out and bite you at some point in the future. Denying the source of your discomfort does not make a problem go away. It just pushes the issue underground where it builds up an opposing force to correct the imbalance in some sneaky way. Eventually the psyche must create an act of enantiodromia to heal your lopsidedness.

Use your journal to make a list of everything about your life that you might be denying. Be absolutely blunt with yourself. This task is tricky, rather like Psyche gathering the fleece, because we're often afraid to approach these dangerous aspects of ourselves directly. Moreover, if we're denying our problems, how can we even be conscious enough to know that they are at issue?

So do as Psyche did. Approach them indirectly. List those

areas of your life where you regularly experience problems or an emotional push-pull response, for within them, your denied parts may be hiding. For instance, if your job is always on your mind, are you telling yourself how much you love it, without giving enough energy to the parts of it that are not gratifying? If your relationship is always in trouble, consider whether you are loving your partner in a worshipful way, without letting yourself feel the aspects of this person that disappoint you. Here's a hint: What you deny is often an aspect of your shadow side.

Ask yourself:

- What could be the shadow part of this issue I'm dealing with?
- Is there something here about myself that I've been unwilling to accept and love?
- Am I seeing only one side of some polarity?
- Am I afraid of my passions?

Now ask yourself:

- What did I do, or how did it come to be, that this particular aspect has come into my life?
- Why and how did I attract this person or event to me?
- What is its message for me?

Once these kinds of reflections have helped you identify some issue that is clouding your emotional space, you can use the following meditation to help clear it:

First, meditate on the ideal that you seek in any situation. Use your inner eye to create a vivid image of this ideal—your perfect job, your perfect relationship, your perfect state of health. Visualizing your goal clearly will help counteract denial or any unconscious illusions you may be holding.

Next, clear your heart of any doubt or negativity. When you feel an openness in your chest area, like fresh air flowing through, begin to feel your way deeply into whatever situation you are working on—the pain of it, the pleasure of it, the fear of it, whatever. Just allow yourself to be with the feeling of whatever you need until you are completely present with it.

Finally, open your heart wide and breathe in the emotional quality that represents the ideal you envisioned. Actually bring in the quality you need on the in-breath, breathing in Spirit, the essence of which is pure love. With each breath, start to feel yourself becoming whatever quality you are seeking. Feel it suffusing your body, heart, and mind.

A Note about Daily Practice

By now your spiritual journal may be in daily use, as explained at the end of Task One. Now if you are willing, begin to carry a little book with you at all times. Make the commitment, at least for a while, to note in it every time you experience emotional reactivity—when something hurts your feelings, makes you angry, makes you feel the need to defend yourself or to prove a point. Also note the times you get excessively high and enthusiastic about something. This feeling, too, may signal an emotional imbalance—the way an addiction feels.

Listen to your mind's chatter, and see what you talk to yourself about. By eavesdropping on your habitual thoughts, you can often see what is upsetting you. Once you've identified the patterns, you've brought order to the chaos of the unconscious mind and given yourself a head start on dealing with whatever is bothersome.

When an emotional moment hits, stop right then, or as soon as the situation allows, sit down by yourself, and vent your hurt or anger or strong urge to be proved right in your little book. Say as much as you want to about how you feel. Really pour it out. No one ever has to read what you've written but you. So feel free to say anything you feel like saying, even if it sounds ugly, stupid, or childish. The point of this part of the exercise is to pour out your heart and empty your hurt—to express yourself fully. Anything you can express you can have power over, but anything that remains unexpressed will have power over you. Often it goes into the shadow and bursts out in a tantrum or turnaround that can make you feel ashamed.

Getting something "off your chest" by writing it is very healing for your emotional body. It's more than half the battle. The rest of the task is identifying the source of your pain and seeing if it's still relevant to your life. It may be that your unhappiness is just a habitual response that goes back a long way, something you no longer need. Often we act out emotionally just so that we can notice something and then take responsibility to heal it. But the first step in any healing is bringing the problem to consciousness.

After you have poured out some strong emotion, ask yourself:

- What does this particular circumstance mean to me?
- What lesson is my soul trying to learn?
- How well am I handling the powerful energies that I am experiencing here?
- How might I handle them better?
- How is my timing or rhythm?

Now you can bring your rational mind into the picture, which we'll learn more about in Psyche's next task. It's important, though, to allow yourself just to express pent-up feelings before getting too analytical about them. Only after emotions are safely vented can you start to see the truth of any situation.

To begin the process of analysis, ask yourself:

- What is really bothering me so much that this situation hooked me?
- What need am I trying to meet? To be loved? To look good? To belong? To be right? To get closer? To gain some distance?

Only you know the answers to these questions. Every emotional reactivity we experience gives us a chance to see some part of life or ourselves we've not yet balanced or integrated.

It tells us that we are still feeling some kind of not-okayness about ourselves. Be willing to focus on what makes you feel anger, shame, pride, jealousy, or bitterness. These strong emotions will point to what it is you believe you lack.

Once you've vented your feelings and done some reflecting, write down any insights that you have. And if you've thought of some way this situation might be brought to a peaceful resolution, write that down, too. You may want to decide upon a certain action or plan a dialogue with someone so that you can clear the fog from your mirror.

I am reminded here of one of my favorite quotations from the great yogi Paramahansa Yogananda in *Inner Reflections, 2000*:

Every day look at yourself
in the mirror of introspection.
That is the way you can become flawless
in the spiritual mirror of your soul.

TASK THREE

Containing the Waters of Life

Psyche's accomplishment of the second task did not please Aphrodite. With a cruel smile, the goddess handed Psyche a crystal goblet, saying, "Someone has helped you again. That's clear. But now I'll put your courage to a more dangerous test. Do you see that high mountain? Below its peak, the dark waters of the river Styx well up to cascade into the gorge below. Go at once and fill this goblet to the brim with ice-cold water taken from the middle of the stream at the point where it bursts out of the rock. Return the water to me with speed, or cruel torture will be the consequence."

All her life, through rumor and tale, Psyche had heard of the deadly river Styx and of the devouring dragons who guarded its rushing waters. Psyche raced toward the mountain, intending to climb as high as she could and throw herself off. The steep precipice was guarded by slippery rocks and crags, their edges razor sharp. Beneath the peak, the mountain spewed forth the vile river, which surged through a narrow channel hidden from view, down, down into the valley below.

On either side of the stream, terrible dragons with fiery breath and unblinking eyes guarded the waters. Even the river itself cried out to Psyche in a terrible voice, "Beware! Begone! Take care! Approach and you will surely perish." Paralyzed with fear, Psyche gazed at this awful scene as if transfixed, but could summon no tears. Though still in her body, her senses had grown as cold as death.

But once more, Psyche's peril called up resources she could not have anticipated. A majestic eagle, royal bird of the high god Zeus himself, flew into Psyche's view. "Give me the goblet," commanded the bird, known for its sharp eyes and deadly precision in swooping down onto its prey. Once before, the eagle had been the god's agent. When Zeus had wished to steal a human boy, the lovely prince Ganymede, to be his cupbearer, the eagle had carried Ganymede up to Olympus. On that occasion, Eros had helped Zeus win the boy. Recognizing Psyche as Eros' bride and knowing that she carried his child, now Zeus would return the favor by becoming an eagle and rushing to assist her.

Psyche gladly obeyed the eagle. Snatching the goblet from Psyche's hand, the bird carried it in its strong jaws, swooping between the guardian dragons to the required spot in the stream. But the waters denied even the great bird easy access. So Zeus as the eagle commanded the waters to open, saying to them, "I've come at Aphrodite's bidding!" On hearing this, the waters quieted, the dragons relented, and the eagle dove into the river, filled the crystal goblet to the brim, and delivered it safely back to Psyche.

How should we interpret this task? What is its message for Psyche and for us? Mythology tells us that the river Styx flows in a circular course around the earth where humans dwell. Swift moving and treacherous, the Styx is the river of life and death, rushing from the high mountain peaks into the depths of hell and back. Seen in the light of depth psychology, we might think of the Styx as the human collective unconscious, the powerful floodtide of unprocessed and disorganized images and archetypes, passions and energies, which inspire and inform the individual human imagination. Within these waters is carried all of life's vitality—birth and death, joy and suffering, triumph and disaster, eternal movement, eternal change.

How can anyone enter such a stream and survive? How can the fragile human vessel contain the onrush and not be shattered? What is our right portion of this collective stream? How much can and should we each take on? These are Psyche's questions and ours as we face the third task.

At one level, the third task challenges Psyche to develop an ego container strong enough to hold her growing complexity. The crystal goblet she carries represents the human ego, the vehicle through which Spirit operates in the world. Psyche's container must be sturdy enough to accommodate everything that she is without cracking apart. With each task, both sides of Psyche's dual nature are growing. Her human capacities are maturing, and she is beginning to use her divine abilities as well. In completing the first task, as you recall, she developed grounded discernment. In the second, she gained emotional maturity and the ability to balance the masculine will to action with feminine patience and intuition.

Yet Psyche finds it difficult to acknowledge these changes. Her impulse to suicide when confronted by each new task indicates that she does not understand that she is growing more powerful with each success. She assumes that the industrious ants and the ingenious reed were outside agents, divine helpers sent by some external power to assist her. She does not yet realize that the divine intervention she is receiving arises from her own inner resources. Like all of us, Psyche finds it easy to devalue herself and to play the role of helpless victim. She finds it much harder to stand witness to her own accomplishments and to claim those greater parts of herself that grow out of the divine aspect of her nature. The symbolic details of this third task end this delusion. They teach Psyche to own her own victories and to accept that she deserves whatever help she receives because of who and what she is.

How does the task reveal this? First, we must remember that cups and vessels of all kinds are traditional symbols of the feminine, the receptacle in which new life is engendered. The flowing torrent of the river Styx is symbolically masculine. As the collective unconscious, it carries the generative seeds of all imaginative and creative endeavors. The task that Aphrodite sets for Psyche is to gather the waters and hold them within a fragile goblet, thus giving them form. Psyche, we remember, is pregnant. Symbolically her pregnancy demonstrates in a way that she cannot deny that her container is strong enough to accomplish the task of form making. In a very literal way, the vessel of her woman's body has contained the flow and is forming it into the new life that is growing within her.

Moreover, the help that arrives for Psyche in this instance, the eagle of Zeus, comes to her aid precisely because of who she is. As the bride of Eros, a human who is the beloved of a god, Psyche has rightly attracted divine notice. Zeus sends his eagle, the same agent he employed when another mortal loved by a god, Ganymede, was to be carried upward. In invoking the name of Aphrodite to quiet the waters, the eagle becomes a symbol of the union of masculine and feminine qualities that has begun to develop within Psyche. As her container strengthens to encompass both the inner masculine and inner feminine, both Zeus and Aphrodite come to her aid, because both are elements of Psyche's own inner divinity.

The message for us in this aspect of the task is clear. We, too, need a sturdy ego container, one that will hold up to the stresses of our complex and growing nature. Whenever a new project or idea is gestating within us, we mirror Psyche's condition as she faces this task. Artists and innovators of all kinds are crucibles of creative alchemy, form makers who are struggling to transform and give new shape to some portion of the collective imagination. Like Psyche, they may fear that they will be split apart by the creative energies they are asked to contain. Yet with the aid of their transcendent faculties—discernment, emotional balance, and here, the discriminating bird's-eye vision of an eagle—they can contain whatever portion of the waters of life and death belongs to them and shape it through their endeavors.

Eventually on the path of illumination we all learn, as Psyche does, that there are no outside experts on the road to self-knowledge. Everything we need to know comes to us through direct experience. As we move along our developmental journey, our challenge is to own our accomplishments rather than believing that they result from the intervention of some higher authority—whether spiritual teacher, personal growth counselor, seminar leader, or therapist. When we acknowledge that we are the authors of our own successes, our creative achievements strengthen our sense of who we are, without giving us a swelled head or sending us off on what is rightly called an ego trip.

I remember a Unity minister telling me once that an integrated ego is one of the most dangerous stages of our awakening. At the time, I didn't understand what he meant, but

I soon learned. It was during those days I tasted professional success for the first time. I took in the accolades and began to think and act in some pretty arrogant ways. Unconsciously my ego had taken on an air of being too prominent in the world now to take so much time with the ordinary folk. For instance, when I look back on that time, I realize that I often returned phone calls from people I considered prestigious while tending to ignore calls from those I felt were less important. I was going to the mountaintop, expecting people to follow me there! It wasn't long, of course, before I crashed and burned. Because my ego had integrated enough to enable me to function successfully in my outer life, I had falsely begun thinking that I'd arrived, and I lost much of my meager following. Quite humbly through the years that followed, I learned that my work is right here in the ordinary world with my clients, students, and loved ones who believe in me. I can see that all of us who are privileged to be teachers continue to have issues to work out and are never very far ahead of those we guide. Anything else is just delusion.

In terms of our daily struggles, we might think of the ego container as a set of boundaries that help us decide what to let in and what to shut out, what to take on and what to leave alone. Whenever we are faced with a challenge in our personal or professional lives, we face Psyche's dilemma. Can our ego hold the energy of transformation, mold it, shape it, and give it form? Can we learn to take on only the tasks that are rightfully ours and let the rest go? Or will we be torn apart by our attempt to contain all of the flow?

This is often tricky business, especially for women. Too

often, women sabotage themselves with a pattern of dysfunctional enabling in which they take on too much or are overwhelmed by tasks or problems that do not belong to them. This pattern is evidenced plainly in the world of addiction. Often the partner or friend of a dependent person becomes a shield for that person's risky or self-destructive behavior, telling lies or covering up for the dependent one's failures, or otherwise trying to save him or her from harmful consequences. For these women (and men, too, who fall into this trap), the ego container needs to grow stronger so that it can hold in what rightly belongs to the individual and shut out what does not!

Another container issue we often face is knowing when or to whom it is appropriate for us to spill our emotional reactions. When feelings of anger and disappointment bubble up in us, we may alienate close friends and family members in our drive to express our needs. Self-expression is certainly essential to our healing. As we say in psychotherapy circles, "If you can't feel it, you can't heal it." However, before we vent the strong emotions that are part of our process, we must find the right container. We need to work with someone who understands emotional release work and can contain this energy for us in a safe and therapeutic setting. Otherwise there's a danger that we will inappropriately leak our anger and frustration onto those we love, who might take it on, believing that our problem is theirs to solve or that they are its cause.

We also face Psyche's task when we are confronted by the enormity of human strife and suffering brought home to us daily through the media. Dipping into this stream of images—Kosovo, the Columbine massacre, terrorism, family violence, war, starvation, disaster—brings on collective feelings of disillusionment, anger, and hopelessness. Our strong emotional reaction to these images is not always just personal but can come as well from the grief of humanity's collective soul confronting its larger-than-life shadow. Carl Jung reminds us that we cannot separate from our archetypal roots any more than we can separate from the organs in our bodies. We are always part of the whole. When some part of humanity suffers, each of us suffers as well. When the archetypal shadow rises, we fear, like Psyche, that our human vessel is too fragile to encompass what it is being asked to hold.

At the surface of our psyches we may feel ourselves to be self-contained individuals. But at our deepest source, we are the world. Society's troubles inevitably trigger archetypal responses, and issues larger than any one person rise like steam from the boiling waters of the river Styx, raging to come out of denial so that they can be owned and healed. The public trial of O.J. Simpson, the Bill Clinton/Monica Lewinsky fiasco, and the heart-wrenching family saga of Elian Gonzales so captivate us because they play out human dramas that must come to the surface of consciousness before they can be released. But the question remains, how much can we bear? How much can any single human vessel safely contain?

The human body is finite. It can hold only so much of humankind's stuff without suffering damage. Those of us who know ourselves to be the sensitives of the world are affected all too easily by the human suffering that is the subtext of world events. Sometimes we don't know the appropriate way to deal with the flood. Psyche's message to us is to be careful to take on only what is ours to work with. Like her, we must develop the eagle-eyed precision and confident clarity to scoop up the portion that is ours and leave the rest alone. If we take on too much, we become helpless and impotent. But dipping into the waters of life and death at just the right spot can provide the raw inspiration to further our personal spiritual and creative goals. The filmmaker who turns the horrors of tribal warfare into a riveting documentary, the social activist who founds a shelter for battered women in one neighborhood in one large city, the family that adopts one abandoned child, have rightly taken on their just portion of humanity's collective sorrow. Because they have been judicious and let in only what is appropriate, their service and their creativity can be of genuine benefit to themselves and to the world at large.

The faculty we need in order to take on only our right portion is discriminating vision. Just as the first task taught Psyche to embody the grounded energies of earth, and the second to use the patient and intuitive emotional qualities of water, this third task teaches Psyche to use her mental faculties, associated with air. The eagle, king of the air realm, is a perfect symbol for her growing mental powers. The eagle in us can rise above any confused human situation and see the bigger picture with farseeing clarity and emotional balance. Eagle eyes can help us see beyond any myopic point of view that might bias us into taking wrong action.

As an aspect of the developing psyche, the eagle represents what I call observer consciousness. Once our emotions begin to balance, the observer consciousness that is part of our innate equipment naturally begins to function. Its task is to keep us centered and at home in our true self. I have always thought of my Observer Self as the mind of my soul. I envision it sitting on my right shoulder, watching what I do with loving concern and nudging me gently, and with absolutely no judgment, anytime I stray from the path. The observer shines the light of awareness on anything that isn't quite right. It's the source of those moments that we call *Aha!*'s when a pattern of relationships becomes clear, or a previously hidden connection jumps into focus. It watches our process as it unfolds, making our life conscious moment by moment. Its discriminating vision stops us between an action and a reaction and offers us the choice between our habitual responses and a fresh approach to life's challenges. It gives us the precious opportunity to be in the world and not of it.

For instance, when one of my client's stepdaughters was nineteen, she started reacting to their house rules with temper tantrums. Though her mother's tendency might have been to respond to these disruptions with anger, her observer consciousness kicked in and offered a more farseeing perspective. During one of these outbursts, she heard her detached observer voice say, "Just be still. She knows it's time for her to be out on her own, yet she's afraid to leave the comfort and protection of the family nest. These tantrums are her way of making you so angry that you will throw her out, since it's too difficult for her to leave on her own." Sharing this insight with her stepdaughter led to a powerful, truthtelling conversation and to a family healing. From that point on, they began to talk about how she might leave home gracefully, and the tantrums ceased.

Through conscious observation, our mental life can become the tamer of our emotional shadow. It can awaken us and keep us on our toes. The observer within helps us stop swinging from one emotional extreme to another, for it shows us rather quickly the right action in any situation. When we bring eaglelike sight into our lives, our minds engage in an ongoing dialogue with our hearts so as to counter the shadow's many voices that keep us debilitated by extremes of neediness and fear. Through conscious self-creative observation, our positive human nature gradually unites with our godlike side, and we are able to look ourselves squarely in the eye, in the truth of our being.

There's a big lesson in this: thought is creative! Your thoughts create your reality. Think about what this truth means in your life. How do you use your mind? Have you ever spent a day or even an hour being conscious of your thoughts? Are there patterns of habitual negativity, assumptions you accept as accurate about yourself or about others, ways that you devalue yourself, or other destructive or debilitating thought tapes that run continually in your head? If so, put your observer consciousness on notice to watch for these patterns and to alert you to their presence. When you become aware of them, gently steer your thoughts in healthier directions, toward noticing your accomplishments, the many joys and beauties of your life, the divinity that resides at your core.

In terms of the chakra system we have been unfolding, Psyche's third task is designed to awaken and heal the third chakra, located at the solar plexus. The energies of the third chakra relate to our personal power in the world and to our ability to form a self or ego that differentiates us as an individual from the socially approved identity we have inherited on the basis of family or "tribal" expectations.

It's easy to know when our third chakra is activated. We're all familiar with the uneasy butterflies we get in the stomach when our self-identity is threatened. Related to the mental body, the third chakra challenges us to develop self-esteem and self-respect, independence and confidence in facing and overcoming life's obstacles. With the observer consciousness as our guide, we learn during this stage of the journey to let go of personal attachments and fears and apply logic objectively anytime it's needed.

The details of the third task are perfectly suited to awaken these faculties in Psyche. The waters of the river Styx were reputed to be poisonous to all who approached them. As long as Psyche's mind accepted this description as fact, her task was apparently hopeless. Only when she enlarged her field of vision and called upon her developing mental powers could she rise above her fears and see a way to accomplish what was needed. In completing the task, Psyche learns that she is capable of thinking creatively for herself beyond the norms of accepted opinion.

The third-chakra phase of our awakening is the time of ego integration. An integrated ego balances the personal and transpersonal aspects of our being—reason and passion, head and heart—and can surrender to the Divine. It helps us relate properly to others, either interpersonally through the engagement of our love nature, centered at the fourth chakra at the heart, or transpersonally, as we open to the spiritual chakras at the throat, third eye, and crown. Through this third task, Psyche completes the triad of the three lower, or personal, chakras: the survival instinct of the first chakra; the balanced emotionality of the second; and here, with the third, a comprehensive sense of personal identity and power. This triad of energies provides the necessary stability for all higher functioning. A healthy ego is the prerequisite for any relationship—whether with another human being or with the Divine.

For Psyche, of course, the relationship that matters most is both human *and* divine—the drive to be reunited with her god-husband Eros. The maturation of Psyche's love for Eros gives her the courage to persevere beyond her wildest expectations. No goddess could ever develop the stout heart of a human woman in love. True love, we're beginning to see, is the key to our continual transformation—not just abstract, universal love, such as archetypes express, but down-to-earth human love that can actually be experienced between individuals.

To gain spiritual stature while in mortal form, we must

undergo many ordeals. Their purpose is to help us know ourselves and to realize that we participate in all of life's forces, both the oh-so-human ones and those that we consider divine. Though in our surface awareness we're not always aware of the deeper meaning of what's happening to us, life requires that we take on countless experiences, high and low, wonderful and terrible, so that we can learn what we are made of. Even as we are whirled about by what feels like capricious fortune, we can be sure that no matter how difficult the challenges we face, the keynote of our human struggle is *always* love.

It is love that is guiding Psyche to discover that women can use the qualities of the masculine principle without becoming masculine themselves. The masculine way is exacting, direct, forceful, and to the point. The feminine way implies a gentle acceptance of what is and a quiet willingness to pursue, so that everybody wins. It is said that the hero fights the dragon to conquer it. The heroine knows how to befriend the dragon and rides peacefully on its back. Psyche is developing not as a male hero would but through a gentle feminine conscious wholeness that never seems to fail her.

Though it may seem that Psyche is out there alone as she faces her terrible tasks, she is striving on behalf of Eros as well. The masculine skills she is gaining belong also to Eros, though neither knows it consciously. Given how the collective mind works, we might say that Eros fled from Psyche for a deeper reason than having been betrayed. On a soul level, he knew that while they were separated, Psyche would complete her human tasks and grow into her goddess stature on her own. For isn't it only through our own direct experience that we can ever know anything at all?

Remember, Psyche and Eros began their archetypal love affair in that elementary stage of consciousness called the participation mystique. In order to evolve toward their true and joint destinies, each must grow in consciousness so that individual love and personal relationship replaces anonymous, universal love. As Psyche matures through her labors of love, so does Eros. The masculine, we are being shown, can be transformed only with and through connection with the feminine. Psyche's tasks bring both to that stage of consciousness wherein the play of opposites is a felt experience. Love and hate, consciousness and unconsciousness, courage and fear, light and dark, masculinity and femininity, humanity and divinity—these polarities must conflict with each other in order to be seen and known. Light cannot be seen until it strikes an object. As we'll see in Task Four, Psyche's betrayal of Eros and her fervent journey to reunite with him moves both toward the highest form of conscious relatedness. As Psyche completes each task, she apprehends new aspects of Eros' reality. And with each, she becomes more and more ready to be the partner of a god.

Take some time now to reflect on how this third task relates to you.

■

Using the Powers of Concrete and Abstract Mind

Some of us are more attuned to the abstract way of seeing things. We apprehend complex events or patterns of relationship in their wholeness, all at once. Or we see right through things and are aware primarily of their deeper meaning and purpose. This way of using our minds can be a real blessing. It keeps us from getting caught up in the details of every little personal incident. Because we see the big picture, abstract thinking can help us identify which issues are ours and which we should avoid. The pitfall of abstract thinking, however, is that it keeps us so far removed from the process of living that we feel ourselves to be above it all. Others may find us aloof or feel that we lack relatedness or compassion.

Abstract thinking can never replace being grounded in reality by a mind that thinks concretely. If you are basically a philosopher type, or highly intuitive, you may gloss over the details of a situation when someone is telling you something, getting the meaning of the event but ignoring the specifics. Later you may realize that you are missing important facts, because you didn't focus on them. Was it the aunt or the cousin who had the car wreck? Did it happen before Emily got sick, or afterward? Did Jerry quit his job, or did he get fired? When we can't concentrate on concrete matters, a vagueness exists in our relationships that can be interpreted as not caring. When we cannot report the facts of an incident correctly, we may even be accused of lying.

To bring balance to our mental lives, we must learn to use both abstract and concrete thinking intelligently and in a timely fashion. And we must be dead honest with ourselves about how much of the "waters" of the human condition we can realistically contain in our one small vessel. Psyche's tasks underscore the importance of this balance:

- We need the concrete mind to analyze facts based on the past or on experience. Concrete thinking helps us bring order to our lives. It separates, divides, compares, sorts, and decides on the appropriateness of things, as we learned with Psyche in Task One.
- Concrete reasoning also must be linked appropriately to the emotions. When our emotions are out of control, we feel confused and often cannot think of what to do. When reason is cut off from the emotions, on the other hand, our responses can be too cold and calculating, divorced from the humanizing effect of feelings. We learned this balance with Psyche in Task Two.
- To balance the concrete mind, we also need the comprehensive vision made possible by abstract thinking. The abstract mind sees life in all its symbolic aspects. From its higher viewpoint, as the eagle demonstrates in Task Three, we can see the whole river of life rushing by and see our appropriate portion of it.

Close your eyes and take a moment now to adopt this eagle-eyed viewpoint on your life. Where are you in this river of human experience? What are you here to do and be? Have you taken on too much or too little? How well are you balancing the masculine and feminine principles within yourself? With the eagle's clear objectivity, enter into the river of experiences and scoop out exactly what's yours to deal with or express at this particular time in your life.

Now take some time to notice the quality of your life, its flavor or color. Sense what it means to be you in the personal reality you call "my life" and how you are doing with it all. Take a moment to reflect on the state of your primary relationships. Are you in love? Have you ever been? Do you know the difference between love and infatuation? If so, how?

As you reflect, notice what parts of your life jump out at you as being the most significant and the most joyful. Which parts turn you on and make you want to get out of bed every morning? Which parts make you feel disempowered, drain your energy, or seem problematic? Use the eagle-eyed perspective of abstract thinking to view these aspects of your life all at once. Make some general statements to yourself that describe your life situation.

Now move down into your concrete mind and think about your situation more specifically. Bring to mind those events that have current energy or interest for you. Notice what these are.

Choose one of the events in which you have a lot of energy, and let's do a little work with it. With your eyes closed, see yourself actually engaging in the activity or event that is attracting your attention. Ask yourself:

- Why am I so drawn to this particular event?
- What am I attempting to achieve?
- What skills or qualities am I using here?
- What skill or attribute that I am missing might help me achieve this goal more easily?

Now dive into your psyche and scoop up this missing skill from the river of life where all potential is churning. Place it in a chalice and pour it into your heart. Feel this missing quality or skill really coming into your body. Use your creative imagination to make this visualization seem like a real happening!

Stand up and walk around for a few moments as though you now possess this new skill or attribute. Explore what it feels like to have it and anchor this feeling in your mind and heart.

Recognize that your identity has begun to shift because of this new skill or attribute. Notice this shift and accept this new identity with an "I am" statement.

Now close your eyes for a moment and honor your mind's way of being both abstract and concrete, impersonal and personal. See your two minds lovingly holding hands over the chasm of your heart, creating a bridge.

A Note about Daily Practice

You can learn to walk every day in the worlds of your Observer Self and of the self who is completely involved in life's conditions. I call this dual vision the practice of self-remembrance. First, you observe what you are doing, moment by moment. Second, you use the perspective of the Observer Self to alter your course, if need be, to refocus on what you spiritually intend.

Commit to going through your day with your Observer Self as your conscious companion, and see what you learn. Remember that any kind of emotional reactivity is a clue that something in you needs to be addressed—a need that is going unmet or an illusion you are caught up in. Use your journal to reflect on these occurrences.

This practice helps you open your heart and surrender your mind to love. For once you see yourself plainly through the eyes of your nonjudgmental Observer, you gain a deeper love for yourself, and therefore more compassion for others.

The open heart is the bridge into the higher realms of human functioning. But the heart cannot open until it is balanced with a clear, nonjudgmental mind. "Work of the eye is done; now go and do heartwork," says poet Rainer Maria Rilke. This is your command, too, as you move into the realm of Spirit.

TASK FOUR

Descending to the Underworld

In fairy tales there are usually three tasks. Psyche is given four. In the science of numerology three is the number of creation; four signifies wholeness or manifestation and grounds creation in the physical plane. In her first three

tasks Psyche had helpers from the animal and plant king-
doms—unconscious aspects of herself represented by earth,
water, and air, the elements that make up the physical, emotional, and mental bodies. In completing these tasks, Psyche
learned to use various aspects of her inner masculine—discernment, emotional balance, and discriminating vision.

In this final stage of her initiation, Psyche enters the mystery of the inner feminine, as represented by the great goddess in both her light and dark aspects. As we recall, Psyche's
plight began when the subjects in her father's kingdom mis-
took the human girl for the heavenly goddess of love and
beauty and worshipped Psyche instead of Aphrodite. As she
nears the end of her sacred journey, Psyche once again faces
the question of whether she is mortal or divine. This fourth
task teaches her that she is at once both human *and* divine
and prepares her to fulfill at last her sacred function as the
new Aphrodite. The path to this new understanding is harrowing indeed. Before Psyche can embody her mature and
queenly feminine nature, she must confront the dark feminine, represented by Persephone, the queen of the underworld, and claim the qualities of divine love and beauty as
her own.

And so our tale continues. Nearly exhausted herself, her
voice worn thin, Aphrodite whispered her next mandate to
Psyche. "Go straight away to the world below. There you must
get from Persephone, queen of Hades, a box of her beauty
ointment. And see that you return it to me at once, for I am
weary from caring for my pitiful son and dealing with the

miserable likes of you! Before I can appear in public this very night, I must anoint my face with some of Persephone's beauty. So be off with you! Do not fail me, or you know the consequences."

Though Aphrodite's other tasks were potentially deadly for Psyche, nothing could be more direct than this. There was no mistaking it. To fulfill this task, Psyche must die. Hearing Aphrodite's words, Psyche remembered the ominous oracle given to her father that she should be married to Death. It seemed the prophecy would come true after all. To Hades she must go, and quickly.

In light of this challenge, Psyche's impulse to suicide when confronted by each of the previous tasks makes sense. Then, in her hopelessness and despair, death seemed the only escape. Yet for the immature Psyche, death would have been a retreat, an unconscious denial of the inner growth necessary to complete the task. Now in this fourth task, death offers no retreat, no denial. Death itself is the task. What Psyche must do is to encounter Death consciously and with purpose.

Though Psyche does not realize it, Aphrodite, the love goddess of the heavenly realms, and Persephone, the queen of the underworld, are two sides of the same divine feminine archetype. As the human link between these two aspects of the Great Mother, Psyche must discover that mature femininity encompasses both light and dark, creation and destruction, love and death. To learn this lesson, Psyche must venture into the deep, inward places where the extremes of beauty and ugliness swim together in paradoxical chaos. There she will realize that only when we face both the luminous and shadowed aspects of existence is it grounded in reality. Maturity requires that Psyche confront her unprocessed illusions—glamour, fear, hopelessness, all the fragmented parts of herself—and reclaim them consciously in love. The idealistic innocence that once sustained Psyche will die in the world of the dark feminine where Persephone is queen.

At the final stage of our journey into spiritual maturity, our illusions must die as well. Should we retreat into innocence and deny either the light or the dark sides of ourselves, we are not complete. In order to grow into our full humanity, we must each in our own way undergo the descent into the underworld to retrieve all in us that is still unconscious and unredeemed. These can be some negative aspects we've denied because we are ashamed of them. Or conversely, they can be certain talents or gifts of the spirit we've not been willing to take responsibility for.

In myth, the descent into the underworld comes in many forms: the hero or heroine is dismembered, or swallowed by a monster or whale, or passes through tunnels or caves, or journeys to the bottom of a sea. In our own psychic life, the descent may come as a period of depression following the death of a relationship, as the loss of a job or other security, as an encounter with a life-threatening illness, or hitting bottom in a devastating addiction. However it manifests, the descent is always fraught with peril, but it can bring about a complete reorganization of our personality. To go up, we must first go down. To grow, those parts of ourselves that no longer serve us must die. Skip this harrowing step, and we risk being trapped in a state that feels like transcendence but is, in fact, premature. Undertaken consciously, the downward journey teaches us to see love and beauty everywhere, even in suffering and decay. Descent, sacrifice, and transformation are the sacred triad that makes any initiation purifying and life changing. As our guide during this final trial, Psyche will undergo all three.

After leaving Aphrodite, Psyche headed straight for a high tower she knew was nearby, and planned to throw herself headlong to a quick and painless demise. But when she arrived at the tower, to her amazement, it spoke to her in a firm but loving voice. "My dear Psyche, why do you fear such a task as this, the very last of all your perils? You have learned so much. Do not lose hope. I will guide you, and you will not fail. Give ear to my instructions, for I know this journey well."

Built by human hands, the tower is a symbol of human consciousness. Its lofty perch represents the summit of the world's cultural and spiritual achievements. In olden days, we might surmise, the tower was a place of refuge for initiates in training, a halfway house between earth and heaven where initiates could be protected while they aligned their mortal powers with a sacred purpose. Though Psyche can learn from the experiences of other seekers, as she does through the tower's advice, she must undertake the perilous journey herself and alone. No animal can help her. No god can intervene. Like all initiates of the mysteries, Psyche must go down into the dark in order to be reborn to new life.

The tower told Psyche of a hidden opening to the underworld through which she must pass. "As you enter," the tower continued, "you must carry in each hand a cake of barley and mead and, in your mouth, two coins to pay for your passage across the river Styx and back. Most important, you must not allow anything to distract you from your course. A lame driver on a three-legged donkey will ask for your aid in picking up some fallen twigs, but you must refuse. Pass on in silence until you meet Charon, the ferryman, who will ask for a toll. Offer him one of the coins, allowing him to take it from your mouth with his own hand. And do not flinch, but pay him your deepest respects."

As she crossed the river, the tower continued, Psyche would see a near-dead man floating in the water who would stretch out a rotting hand and beg her to lift him into the boat. For this suffering man as well, the tower warned, she must have no pity but ignore his plea and continue on her way. On the other side of the river, she would meet three weaving women who had lost their needle in a stack of hay. They will implore her to help them, saying that they are weaving the web of fate to save the world. But once more, Psyche must not give them aid, but continue with focused intent toward her goal.

Each of these encounters will try to tempt Psyche away from her purpose by appealing to her natural feminine pity and compassion. It's hard for us to hear that we must sometimes close our hearts toward those in obvious need. But like every initiate, Psyche's concentration must be single pointed, her attention focused solely on her greater goal. Psyche's ego strength she has garnered during her last task will here be put to the test. Can she stay true to her spiritual quest and avoid falling into an excess of softhearted relatedness?

The natural wish to help can be, for many people, a trap that compromises their ego stability and threatens to enmesh them in concerns that deflect them from their high intentions. The woman who sacrifices her own life to spend years caring around the clock for an infirm parent, or the father who jeopardizes his own financial security to rescue an adult child from the consequences of bad judgment have fallen into the precise pitfall Psyche is warned against. Those of us who consider ourselves to be feeling types are easily distracted by the suffering of others. We must learn to stay focused on our bigger story and not get snared by every painful condition we encounter. Codependence robs us of our ability to be rational and wise. Remembering that rescuers continue to be responsible for those they save can, perhaps, turn us away from the self-defeating habit of enabling.

"Next," the tower told her, "you will meet Cerebus, the three-headed dog that guards the gates of Hades. You must appease him by throwing him one of the pieces of barley cake you hold, saving the other to throw to him on your return." In myth, dogs often represent the instinctual drives of the lower self. Here, the dog's three heads represent our physical, emotional, and mental needs. The lesson for Psyche in this detail is that by judiciously feeding each part of ourselves the proper amount of the right stuff at the right time, our cravings will subside, and our life passages will be safe and untroubled.

The tower continued: "These are all the goddess's snares, set deliberately to deter you from your goal. Look straight ahead, Psyche, and keep to your mission, no matter what! You must continue until you reach the doorstep of Persephone's palace. She will welcome you kindly and offer you a fine meal while she prepares the beauty ointment you have asked for. Do not sit at the table with the goddess, nor eat any of her food. Remember, you are a human girl! Sit upon the ground as a servant would and take only coarse bread and water for your sustenance. After you dine in this fashion, in deepest gratitude and with a humble bow, take your leave, carrying with you the sealed box of beauty ointment the goddess will give you.

"Upon your return, feed the three-headed dog the remaining cake and offer the ferryman the last coin. Then proceed, retracing your steps, until you return to the starry night sky at the place where you started."

Here the tower paused, and its voice sounded a note of ominous warning. "There is one more thing you must remember, Psyche. Do not, under any circumstances, open Persephone's jar! The treasure of divine beauty within is entirely forbidden to you. Remember, you are a human girl, not a goddess.

"So now, Psyche, you are thoroughly prepared. Be on your way. Follow my instructions to the letter, dear girl, and do not weaken for even a moment!"

Armed with the tower's instructions and motivated by her deep yearning for Eros, Psyche embarked upon the heroine's journey into the underworld. So immersed was she in the details of her task that its ultimate purpose seemed beyond her awareness, yet she moved ahead, remembering each instruction, completing each step, never giving way to fear or despair. Psyche's actions here remind us that the Soul Events in our lives are always unfolding our greater story and moving us forward, even when the day-to-day details of life seem to be taking us in the utterly wrong direction! On some deep level Psyche knew that her destiny was being fulfilled. Her dedication is a message of hope to all seekers of wisdom and true love! How often have you heard yourself say, after some destiny-shifting event has occurred, "I just knew this was going to happen!" Yes, it's true. Something in you always knows.

The events of the journey unfolded exactly as the tower foretold. Each test gave Psyche the opportunity to demonstrate that she had assimilated a lesson from the first three tasks. When she passed the lame driver and his donkey, she exercised discernment—the lesson of the first task—in refusing to be drawn in by a request from someone who expects others to do his work. When she ignored the half-dead man in the water, she showed that she was in control of her emotional responses, which she had learned during her second task. When she ignored the plea of the weavers, she demonstrated that she knew her limitations—the lesson of the third task—and understood that no one can interfere with the web of fate. Though her heart was filled with compassion, she was focused on her own goal. Psyche teaches us here that only when we ignore unconscious or unclean motivations and refuse to succumb to them does our destiny unfold according to plan.

Arriving at Persephone's palace, Psyche refused a place at the goddess's table and ate her simple meal on the floor of the kitchen while Persephone prepared the ointment. Psyche's humility represents her unveiling—the stripping away of all pretence. Death is a great leveler. When we face our own mortality, all illusions die. There comes a time in every initiatory event when we are "disrobed" as a prelude to the moment when our inner beauty shines forth from the soul.

Persephone is the perfect final teacher for Psyche. She, too, was once a carefree young girl, daughter of Demeter, goddess of nature. Kidnapped by Hades and taken to the underworld to be his bride, Persephone understands what it means to live in both the heights and the depths of feminine experience. For six months every year, Persephone reigns in the cold world of death while on earth the harsh winds of winter mourn her passing. But when six months of cold have been endured, to fulfill a bargain between Hades and Demeter, Persephone returns to earth, bringing with her the warm breezes of springtime. A profusion of wild flowers celebrates her annual return to the land of the living.

This divided life gives Persephone deep wisdom. Better than anyone, she knows that nature moves in cycles and that winter always gives way to spring. By her queenly presence, she demonstrates that it is possible to rise above the vicissitudes of life's fortunes and to cope with its inevitable ups and downs without bitterness at one's fate. Persephone's story speaks of the tranquility that comes from mirroring the natural rhythms of the earth. As Psyche gazed at life through

Persephone's eyes, she saw that the mature soul is able to stay present even in the midst of paradox and to ride life's changes with serenity and grace. And she began assimilating Persephone's wisdom.

Persephone also represents the transition from maiden to wife. Before her abduction, she was, like Psyche, unaware of her own desires and strengths. Yet the Persephone that Psyche meets has grown into a great queen, a mature goddess who reigns over a vast kingdom and claims what she wants for herself. The transformation from innocent maiden to wife is exactly what Psyche faced. In her immature union with Eros, marriage just happened to Psyche, as it had to Persephone, at the whim of the gods. The mature Persephone models for Psyche that though a maiden might be swept away into marriage, she can grow into an adult acceptance of the role of wife and transform from a *puella aeternus*, or eternal maiden, to a woman worthy of full partnership with a divine husband.

Moreover, in her marriage to Pluto, Persephone fulfilled the fate that had been decreed by the oracle for Psyche. Persephone had married Death indeed! Yet she was not destroyed by it. Through her suffering she has become wise to the ways of the world. Conscious suffering always leads to growth. All this Psyche learns from Persephone, as can we. The dark side of the Divine Feminine has much to offer us, if we bow to her grace.

With the tightly sealed jar safely in her possession, Psyche retraced her steps and returned to the living world. Yet one more test, perhaps her most difficult, awaited her. As she traveled swiftly to Aphrodite's palace, her longing for her beloved Eros was so strong that she could actually feel his arms around her and hear his sweet voice. So, as any woman might do, she paused for a moment by a pool of fresh water to wash her dirty face and rearrange her hair for this long-desired reunion. But when she saw her reflection in the water, her eyes filled with tears. How could she face Eros looking so travel worn and bedraggled? Wouldn't he turn away in disgust, horrified at what had happened to his sweet, young bride? But then, suddenly and with a shiver, she remembered the special ointment that she held in her hand. And she thought, "Surely I can borrow just a little of Persephone's ointment for myself. If I anoint my face with a bit of this divine beauty, my lord will find me irresistible, for then I'll be as a goddess myself and fit to be his bride!" And with that thought and no other, she opened the jar. But then, horror of horrors! Though the box appeared to be empty, out flew a great cloud of noxious sleep wrapping Psyche in a deathlike slumber. And there she lay as though a corpse, her life force seemingly extinguished at the hour of her greatest triumph.

What shall we make of Psyche's new disobedience? Had she succumbed to vanity and forgetfulness, all her efforts for naught? Or was there a higher purpose that her actions served? On one level, the sleep into which Psyche fell reminds us of the death-in-life state of the unwed princesses in many fairy tales. Like Snow White having eaten the poison apple, or Sleeping Beauty, her finger pricked by the enchanted needle, Psyche's sleep appears to trap her in perpctual girlhood, the consummation of a mature and conscious reunion with Eros forever beyond her reach. Yet like her earlier disobedience with the lamp, Psyche's actions were the kind of mistake known as a *felix culpa*—which means "a happy sin"—that pushes one toward a greater good. When she falls asleep, she dies to her immature identity. This is the kind of sleep that precedes a shift in consciousness from one state to another.

In the teachings about initiation from every spiritual tradition, we're told that in order to be transformed, we cannot be attached to anything at all, even to our own salvation. All must be sacrificed for a higher good. The maiden in Psyche must be sacrificed before the wished-for transformation to wife can take place. Psyche's sacrifice mirrors the wisdom of nature, the lesson of Persephone's story—that death must precede rebirth into new and greater forms. Both are part of the cycle of reality. And though we would certainly prefer it, and no matter how clever we are, we cannot avoid the death part, as our new life depends on it.

The word *sacrifice* comes from the Latin word *sacer*, which means "to make holy." When we make a sacrifice, we offer up all that we hold dear, not knowing what, if anything, we will gain by our deed. We simply wait, as though dead, until some act of grace or new vision arrives. In our work at Eupsychia, we call this in-between place "hanging in the dangle." Life often presents us with situations in which we hang suspended, like a trapeze artist who has let go of one swing and turned in midair to await the arriving swing, with nothing to sustain him but faith. The old way is dead, but the new way has not yet arrived, and that's just how it is. No act of will can get us past this place. All we can do is make our suffering conscious, examine our faith, and remain steady in the nothingness.

Yet Psyche's sacrifice has another meaning as well. Seen in the light of her search for self-knowledge, her act of disobedience is an assertion of her right to be a goddess and to seize divine beauty for herself. When she was a young girl, divine beauty was ascribed to Psyche by the subjects in her father's kingdom. Yet Psyche had never inhabited that beauty, never claimed it as her own. Now she was ready to do so. In opening the box, Psyche was saying in effect, "This belongs to me." Moreover, her motivation in claiming divine beauty for herself was not selfish vanity. Instead, it was love—healthy self-love and love for Eros, her masculine half, the being who would complete her and make her whole. Divine beauty is love made visible. In anointing herself with divine beauty, Psyche announced her willingness to enter into personal love and to raise it to the level of the sacred. As we will see, her disobedience was no mistake but represented the highest courage, a surrender to love that motivated Eros to rise from his sickbed to come to her aid. When Psyche awakened from her deathlike sleep, she would no longer be the young girl she was but a mature and conscious woman, ready to take her rightful place at the side of a god.

Psyche's sacrifice for the sake of divine love and beauty represents the opening of the heart chakra, the gateway to the three upper, spiritual chakras that hold the powers of creative imagination, inspiration, and intuitive wisdom. The fourth chakra bridges earthly and spiritual ways of being. Its opening ignites in us the element of fire, the spiritual aspect of our nature. We need not focus on the three higher chakras directly. When our hearts are open, the qualities of chakras five, six, and seven, when needed, just naturally come alive in us. Our creative imagination awakens; we become easily inspired; and our intuition, honed to a precise degree, recognizes the truth of every situation. The open heart is like a magnet that unifies all opposites, ripening us for marriage at every level: the inner marriage of self and soul, the earthly marriage to a human beloved, and the divine marriage between our questing soul and its Source.

Throughout her adventure, Psyche's actions were motivated by love, but until this moment in the story, her understanding of love's power was incomplete. She did not understand that the heart's authentic quality is not indiscriminate compassion, as many believe. By focusing on her love for Eros and not allowing herself to be sidetracked into generalized compassion, Psyche opened the eye of her heart, which sees all things in truth. With this inner eye, she saw for the first time the truth of her own nature, and motivated by her open heart, she claimed her right to divine love and beauty. In doing so, Psyche proved that she was courageous enough to enter into partnership with Eros as his equal and so fulfill her sacred destiny.

Still closeted in his mother's bedroom, Eros felt the opening of Psyche's heart and sensed her peril. Until Psyche, Eros had known love only as a boy's wanton game of sensual desire. As Psyche's other half, his growth toward mature understanding of the nature of love paralleled hers. We might even say that Psyche had labored on behalf of both. Now, galvanized by love, Eros could endure Psyche's absence no longer. Filled with desire, his heart opened wide, and he slipped out of the window of his sickroom and flew to her aid. With a harmless prick of his arrow, Eros awakened Psyche and gathered her into his arms. Imagine Psyche's joy at opening her eyes and beholding the love and tender concern on the face of her beloved! Whispering a quick word of encouragement, Eros sent Psyche on her way to Aphrodite to fulfill the conditions of her task, while he set out on a mission of his own to win approval for their ultimate union.

Isn't it paradoxical that a mortal must teach an immortal god to love? But seen in the light of the male-female dynamic within ourselves and between men and women, it's not so strange after all. Women are the relationship makers of the world, both in terms of human male-female pairings and in terms of the divine play of forces that make up the universe. The feminine principle represents loving acceptance of every aspect of creation—pain and joy, profane and sacred, separation and union. It is the task of the feminine to blend these opposites into a new and greater whole containing the best of each and to move beyond this joining toward the transcendence of all duality.

The Eros who flew to Psyche's side was no longer the silly boy nursing his wounded pride in his mother's house. The *puer aeternus*, or eternal youth, had deepened into a mature god with the ability to recognize, honor, and serve genuine love. Here in the myth, as so often in real life, it is a woman who mediates this transformation. When the masculine and feminine principles within Psyche were consciously joined, Eros, or love, evolved into its mature and sacred form. Serving its highest function, Eros penetrates our psyches—not with boyish lust but with the Eros principle, the passionate energy that inspires and drives all creative and spiritual endeavors.

No longer content with secret couplings in the dark, Eros was determined to make Psyche a goddess and to bring her to live with him forever in the Olympian realm. While Psyche sped to Aphrodite's palace, swift-winged Eros soared to the heights of heaven to ask Zeus for aid. At first, Zeus chided Eros for the many times the boy's arrows had sent Zeus off on some embarrassing amorous adventure or another. But seeing the change that love had wrought in Eros, Zeus' heart melted with fatherly love, and he quickly agreed to his request. He sent for Psyche and offered her a cup of ambrosia, saying, "Drink this, and you will be immortal. You have earned your place at the side of your husband, who is indeed a god. Your marriage to him will endure forever." A nuptial banquet was laid out, and all the gods and goddesses took their places around the table. Even Aphrodite swallowed her pride and congratulated the happy pair.

Thus did Psyche, a mortal, become the wife of Eros, god of love and inspiration. Soon Psyche gave birth to their daughter, whose name in heaven is Joy, while on earth, she was called Pleasure. Joy is the soul's happiness; pleasure is ecstasy of the physical senses.

psyche's seeds

Though we have looked at many of the themes and lessons of Psyche's fourth task as the story unfolded, let's look in conclusion at what the task as a whole can teach us about our own spiritual journey.

We have said that Psyche's descent to the underworld was an initiation experience. In its traditional sense, initiation implies an expansion of consciousness, an opening of the mind and heart, stage by stage, to a recognition of the inner divinity that is our essential nature. Initiation is an aspect of the formal path of many spiritual traditions. However, in my work, I have encountered many people who feel themselves to be undergoing a process of initiation not connected to formal religious practice. Perhaps you are one of them.

Sometimes an initiation experience comes upon you suddenly, without giving you time to prepare. Without being conscious of having decided to change, you simply start behaving differently. You lose interest in your old ways and shift from being outer directed to seeking guidance from within. Inner reflection becomes your main activity. But be forewarned. Initiation is a voluntary process, but never a choice for the fainthearted! Once you stand at the doorway of initiation, having proven to the gods that you're sincere, a powerful transformative whirlwind will blow away all complacency, and everything that is not based in truth in your life will be swept away.

If you are conscious of being an initiate, you may be keenly aware of the responsibility you hold for your part in making a new and better world. This awareness may take the form of an obsession with unfolding your life's work and true purpose. Initiate consciousness is supercharged with a spiritual intensity and inspiration that won't let up, except when your commitment to some piece of sacred work has been completed. Then you may be able to relax, at least until the next inspiration hits. As the process of initiation unfolds, you outgrow each limited way of being and are reborn into a greater and greater identity until you are complete. At the end of your journey, like Psyche, you know yourself to be immortal, for the divine soul that is your essence never really dies.

The tower that guided Psyche on her journey of initiation does not speak to all who arrive at its doors for refuge from the world. Like a wise spiritual teacher, it guides only those who have taken an internal vow to become initiates through the trials that lead ultimately to their complete unfolding. By choosing first to listen to the advice of the tower but then to disobey its final warning, Psyche models the appropriate relationship of the initiate-in-training to a spiritual guide. Awakening certainly requires wise guidance, but you must also have a mind of your own. We can always seek advice from those we respect, but only adopt it if our inner knower says yes. Initiation invites you to make your own decisions, to stand tall in the light of your own soul and to inhabit fully your Divine Self, perhaps for the first time.

Into what mystery was Psyche initiated? And what can we learn from her experience? The path that Psyche traveled to spiritual illumination is through human/personal love. Here is a high mystery indeed. In her role as mediator between the human world and world of Spirit, Psyche is the link between the divine principle of love and its working out in the world of real relationships between human partners. In disobeying the tower and claiming her right to the beauty secret of a goddess, Psyche brought divine beauty to the human realm. And then, in using this beauty to win the personal love of an immortal, Psyche raised individual, human love to the level of the gods.

And so it must be for us. Love, we are being told, is a divine treasure. Whenever we love another person, we are, in some sense, stealing the treasure of the gods. Psyche's story reminds us that love can be so much more than a way to fulfill the ego's selfish needs for security, belonging, and positive self-identity. It can be a sacred bond and a path to the highest illumination. We humans have the responsibility to sacralize our loving. In return, the gods will humanize their love for us by being as near as our heartbeat and by demonstrating their loving concern for us as individuals. Loving union, as Psyche discovered, must take place on every level. Before we can join with another human being, the masculine and feminine halves of our inner nature must come together. Then our human partnerships, entered into for the right reasons and honored as a sacred mystery, can be avenues to spiritual transcendence.

If you have a partner as you are reading this, don't be afraid to ask yourself why you have chosen your current mate. Was it ego need or was it love? Is your pairing truly "made in heaven"? Does it fulfill the promise of divine love?

If not, what can you do to transform your relationship into love's highest expression, into a sacred mystery? Here are a few secrets you can use to spiritualize your human relationship:

- As you explore your reasons for being with your partner, ask yourself whether and in what ways this pairing fulfills your highest purpose for being on this earth. Acknowledging that your choice of a partner serves a spiritual purpose can help make your relationship sacred.
- Try to see any difficulties in your relationship as spiritual challenges. Make working out your differences with loving respect for both you and your partner an aspect of your daily spiritual practice.
- Practice surrender. A true act of surrender is an actual experience of letting go and letting be. Surrendering to love is not a defeat. Rather, it is softening and opening the heart so that you become more loving and more available to being loved.
- Love your partner's Divine Self. Allow the eye of your heart to open to your partner's essential divinity, especially when the going gets rough. Loving each other High Self to High Self is the way of the gods and a path to heaven on earth.

The union of Psyche and Eros is a love story that can inspire us on every level. Psyche, you remember, is your own twinned soul, which looks both to the Source of all loving and to the very human ways that personal love works itself out in our lives. The union of our human psyche and erotic love is for many people a path to Spirit. What is required is that we keep forever before our eyes the ways that every human coupling reflects the alchemical conjunction of opposites—the sacred marriage, which is the ecstasy every mystic seeks. When we come together with our partner in love, we are, at the highest level, seeking to regain our original sense of wholeness and completion. Sexual union is the joining of heaven and earth, light and dark, yang and yin, active and passive, both between us and our partners and within ourselves. The fruit of such unions, as the story of Psyche and Eros reminds us, is much more than earthly pleasure. It is heavenly joy, the soul's highest and most ecstatic expression blended with earthly pleasure.

So, you see, we have our work cut out for us. Psyche and Eros withdrew from this world to live in the Olympian realms—we might say, in terms of the Jungian archetypal psychology we have been unfolding, in the realm of the collective unconscious. In other words, the human-Divine marriage exists only in potential. It is our task to undertake the journey to retrieve it for ourselves and to bring the mystery of sacred union into our lives.

Psyche accepted the mantle of her destiny. Can we? Can you? Are you willing to go the distance, to die if necessary to your old ways and to tread the path of initiation into the divine mysteries of love? Are you willing to strive as Psyche did to discover and join the divided halves of your inner being and to allow this joining to be reflected in your human relationships? Are you willing to claim the treasure of Divine

Love for yourself? And if you do, are you prepared to do your part in returning love, transformed and humanized, to the gods?

Self-reflection

▩

Opening to the Fires of Imagination, Intuition, and Inspiration

Let's stop for a moment and reflect on how far you've come on your own journey of individuation. Take out your journal and jot down what comes to mind as you read through the following questions:

- Are you in touch with your true mission, your purpose for incarnating here on earth?
- Are you aware of your bigger story? If you were to write it as a personal myth, what kind of story would it be?
- In what ways have you made a descent into the underworld? What were the consequences of this journey?
- In what ways have you become aware that you have both a dark and a light side? How do you see this duality reflected in the world outside yourself, even in the realm of the Divine? How do you feel about this understanding?
- Jot down and reflect on your "big memories"—your significant dreams, inner visions, or Soul Events. Do they follow a pattern or suggest a unified theme? If so, what is your role? What purpose are you here to serve?

- What are you doing in your current life that expresses your spiritual gifts or highest purpose?
- Is the Eros principle active in your life? Do you feel inspired?
- Are you willing to commit to being an initiate and to taking the advice of an inner guide? If not, what blocks you or makes you unwilling to embark on the path?
- Since beauty is love made visible, how much beauty do you see or allow to exist in your life? What might you do to make your life more beautiful?

Now put on some music that opens your mind and heart, and give yourself permission to be very private for a while. Allow yourself to feel who you really are in your spiritual essence, at your very core. Experience this self-remembrance for several minutes.

When you come out of your meditation, allow the self-love you feel to warm your whole body and to relax and release any tightness or holding around your heart.

Spiritual fire is all around us. When our hearts are open, it pours spontaneously through all of our ways of knowing. When divine love has entered us, the doorway to creative imagination, inspiration, and intuition, ruled by the three higher chakras, stands wide open.

The fifth chakra, located at the region of the throat, brings us the creative imagination to see how the images that appear in our dreams and inner visions express as our Highest Self. The sixth chakra, located at the region of the third or spiritual eye between the brows, provides the inspiration that moves us to serve the whole through the insights we gain from higher vision. Here the Eros principle comes alive in us, giving us an erotic passion for life and a strong desire to follow a higher calling. The seventh chakra, at the crown of the head, is where divine intuition or direct knowing penetrates our consciousness. Through this highest energy center, we hear the voice of intuition or God's will and gain a sense of the future.

To experience the energy of these spiritual centers, lift your eyes from the words on this page and let them fall on some object in nature—a bird, a blossom, a tree branch. Using the creative imagination of the fifth chakra, allow this object to open to its spiritual symbolism. For instance, see a flower bud as the promise of future pleasure, or a spider-web as the gossamer threads of connection between you and others.

Now soften your gaze and feel the love you have for this particular creation. At the same time, bring to mind the image of someone or something you love. Allow the inspiration of the sixth chakra's Eros principle to enter your heart. Open to the connections you feel between the symbol you have chosen from nature and the thing or person that you love. Pay attention to what messages about your highest calling come from this connection.

Finally, breathe the love you're feeling up into the crown of your head. Allow this feeling of love to shower down on you and to shoot outward toward all creation and toward the Divine Source of All. Feel that your love is an aspect of divine love and that by loving, you have made divine beauty visible on earth. Stay quiet with this feeling for a while and see what your intuition tells you about love. . . .

Practice this meditation during your walks in nature until it becomes a regular experience in your life. When you've practiced this meditation a few times, you'll notice that anything you look at can open you to this same miracle. You'll be seeing the extraordinary in the ordinary—spiritualizing the material world. This is the experience of living with an open heart, from your center, from your whole self. The secret to spiritual illumination is for us each to be willing to do our part and live this miracle now. Heaven and earth must marry in us. Then we'll be living as the demonstrators of the Divine we all came here to be.

part II

twelve seeds
thoughts for
your journey

Though I do not believe that a plant will spring up where no seed has been, I have great faith in a seed. Convince me that you have a seed there, and I am prepared to expect wonders.

—Henry David Thoreau, *Faith in a Seed*

how to use psyche's seeds

What if a year from now you could look back and see that you're living exactly the life you had always dreamed possible? The transformation you long for can be yours. Each Seed Thought you will study here is a living truth. If you practice it as a spiritual intention, it can change your life. Plant the right seeds, and be prepared to expect wonders!

The Seed Thoughts in this section are not simply intellectual or psychological principles; nor are they drawn from any one of the world's spiritual philosophies. Each has been distilled from my long years of working hands-on with trainees and participants who have come through our training and healing intensives, revealed to us through these men and women in their psychospiritual inner work. I have since set down these findings as the postulates of a spiritual psychology that govern Eupsychia's work, to help our trainees learn to guide others along the same journey they've been willing to travel.

Psychospiritual guides differ from conventional psycho-therapists in that they can only lead their clients into realms they themselves have journeyed within the depths of the psyche. Otherwise they have no experience or credibility to assure their clients that they are safe when they hit some of the harsher labors in their transformational journey. This is why in our work we combine healing ourselves and guiding others as all one process.

Even reading books on psychospiritual truths differs from ordinary reading. The psychological and spiritual messages encapsulated in these Seed Thoughts are layered, such that different aspects of meaning apply to your unfolding at different times. You will hear what you need to hear at the moment as you read a story or explanation, finding that you gain new perspective every time you deepen. The track we follow on our soul's journey is not linear. We travel at various speeds, even cycling back over the same stages of learning in a spiraling fashion, moving deeper and deeper to integrate aspects of a truth we did not fully incorporate on our last pass. As we deepen, our wisdom expands.

If a particular Seed Thought grabs you, it may help you complete a life lesson that is up for you right now. The same may be true if you experience a strong negative reaction. Perhaps the message that repels you points to some aspect of your shadow, some truth about yourself you may be denying or resisting. So take note if something in you rebels strongly at an idea presented here.

Each of the Seed Thoughts corrects a painful illusion about

the self we may have carried since childhood. Depending on how we were raised, some of us will be more sensitive to one kind of issue than to another. These illusions protected us in some way; that is why we retained them. Be patient with yourself. The soul's timing must be right and the personality receptive for psychospiritual truths to penetrate our ego's defenses.

You may find it useful to use these thoughts as daily or weekly meditations, turning to one or another that seems especially apt. Read each slowly as many times as necessary and allow your psyche to savor its meaning. Write it out, draw a symbol representing it, or journal a personal story that it calls up from memory. Dream about it and take the time to hold on to and record your dreams. Devote some time to reflecting on the theme of the Seed Thought, giving it time to positively affect your life.

Seed Thoughts are organic. They must be planted deep and nurtured if they are to take root and grow. They bring about a quickening that happens first in the mind and then in the heart. After working with them for a while, as you're going about your ordinary routines, they'll begin to manifest as changes in what you do and how you look at things.

The exercises that accompany each Seed Thought invite you to experiment with deep reflection or inner work. They have been used by hundreds of men and women in my workshop intensives over the past two decades. These workshops function as living experiments in sacred group work, during which people who participate use these and similar techniques to catalyze great changes in their lives and in the lives of their families.

Psychospiritual learning cannot be taught. It can only be discovered through direct experience. Spiritual exercises give you the opportunity to grow by doing. Many teach you to use the power of visualization, or inner sight, to expand your understanding. If you are new to using visualization techniques, you should know that inner imaging is not seeing pictures as you do with your outer eyes. Inner imagery might be described as the form that a thought takes, a momentary impulse of light or color or shape, a glimpse of memory, a real or imagined scene. Sometimes you won't see, but you will sense something—for instance, a sudden chill or a feeling as if warm water were running up and down your body. And sometimes there will be a direct knowing, with no sensory impression whatsoever. Don't discount whatever comes, no matter how fleeting. The capacity for "in-sight" is inborn. Inner seeing is the way our soul conceives. We only need to be reminded, and then practice makes the skill a reality.

Inner vision, moreover, is not simply a head experience. Whenever you access psyche's visionary powers, your whole body is involved. You can help your body participate in the experience by paying attention to its needs. Lie down or sit in a comfortable position. If music helps you relax or to create images, put on the sound track from a movie or other music without words and let yourself dissolve into the flow of sound. Take a hint from the yogis and focus on the breath for a few moments, allowing your ordinary cares and concerns to exit the body with each out-breath. Give yourself the gift of a few moments with absolutely no agenda and see what arises.

Seed Thoughts are ideas whose time has come. Like the seeds scattered along a winding path in a fairy tale, like the seeds Psyche sorted with newly developed discernment at the beginning of her quest, the twelve Seed Thoughts that follow and their accompanying exercises can change your reality. They can be seeds of wisdom for you—markers along the path on your journey toward wholeness.

Seed Thought One
You are both human and divine; only when both sides of our nature are honored do we thrive.

Recognizing that you are both human and divine is an act of sacred self-remembrance that lays the foundation for everything you aspire to do or to be. Honoring only one side of your nature diminishes both halves of your being.

Like Psyche, many of us begin our journey to consciousness very confused about who and what we are. We should have been taught about our twinned human/divine nature when we were young. However, many of us were raised by parents who believed that the natural human drives toward free expression, feeling, creativity, and sexuality were sinful or wrong. We were taught to be good little boys and girls— to obey, to conform, and never to question. No wonder so many of us grew up with shame, neurotically out of touch with the wonder of our true being. Yet paradoxically, as Psyche had to learn, self-creation sometimes requires that we disobey, that we find a way around the strictures placed on us, that we shine the lamp of consciousness into places our parents and teachers would never have permitted us to venture.

Often the religions in which we were raised reinforced the view that human nature is sinful, teaching us that if we follow our selfish desires rather than what we are told is God's design, we are guilty of disobeying divine laws. How sad this pattern is, and how much effort it takes us in adulthood to correct this mistaken notion! Rejecting our God-given humanity, or labeling its natural desires as selfish or evil, negates the purpose of human incarnation. Far from being sinful or limiting, the drives of the human ego are vital to our development. As the executor of our human personality, a healthy ego knows how to keep us safe and behaving appropriately in the world.

Being taught that human nature is sinful, however, is not the only way children can be damaged in their divine self-perception. Others of us were raised by parents who were entirely secular and rarely thought about God or religion at all. Instead, they programmed us to believe that human nature is purely physical and that the material world and its secular gods of money, fame, and success are all that matters. As a result of this training, many of us learned to exalt the material ego and to worship worldly success. Because our parents did not help us to see our spiritual side, we were taught to prepare for material achievement through becoming better personas, through figuring out which mask to wear to reap the greatest of society's rewards. "Compete and get to the top, no matter what you have to do to get there" was the rule we lived by. All other achievements, including spiritual ones, were viewed as irrelevant or as signs that we had failed.

A sad twist on this materialistic view are those parents who have been part of a pop culture and who believe that free sex and drug use are quite all right, even in front of their children. Children from these families often fail to develop healthy, self-confident egos that deepen in adulthood into spiritual qualities that are nonegoistic, concerned for others, and imbued with a sense of service and sacred purpose.

These limited kinds of upbringing damage the human-divine hybrid that is our essence. In one case, we're taught that our humanness is sinful, and we must deplore it. In the other, the materialist ego is worshipped as our earthly—and *only*—God. Either way we grow up lopsided. Without true principles to guide us, we travel on our soul's journey with much stumbling and much suffering to overcome. An evolving soul is neither exclusively spiritual nor exclusively material. Only when both halves of our nature are honored do we thrive.

The mystical traditions of the world offer teachings that can counter these limited views of human nature. For example, the Gnostic Christian Gospels, those accounts of Jesus' teachings that were buried in the religious politics of Roman orthodoxy, tell a second story of the Last Supper that is not widely known but which was beautifully interpreted by Dr. Stephan A. Hoeller in his book *Jung and the Lost Gospels.*

In it, Jesus asks his disciples to participate with him in a sacred dance, a *chorea mystica* such as was performed in many of the ancient mystical traditions.

The twelve disciples were to surround Jesus as the thirteenth point in the circle and dance their way into the new world. As they danced, they chanted, "I was Beauty and the beautiful; the Baker and the bread; the Lover and the loved one; Sorrow and the one who sorrowed . . ." thus honoring both the archetype and the human experiencer as one, and thereby closing the door to dualism. The dance, Jesus told them, is essential, for "Those who do not know how to dance have missed the point of my incarnation."

On one level, the dance celebrates and honors the duality of Christ's "being in the world and not of it." Yet on another level, the dance carries the message that we, too, can be both fully involved in the spiraling rhythms of life while, at the same time, we participate in life's archetypal and spiritual dimension. Every human being, Jesus was telling us, is simultaneously the archetype and its expression, the Creator and the created, the Divine Soul and its working out in the human life of the world.

There will always be a part of us that must dance our way fully into life. Human existence, with its fiery passions, juicy emotions, and expressive urges is as much a part of our being as are our spiritual longings. There is no desire in us that is harmful if it is mixed with psychological health and an attitude of harmlessness toward others. At the same time, we must acknowledge our divine origins and sacred purpose. As we dance through life, the aspect of our being that comes from Source and journeys toward reunion with the Divine transcends the messiness of human incarnation and keeps us linked and focused on our spiritual goals.

The danger for our soul comes when we become "too human," immersing ourselves in materialistic pursuits and ignoring our soul needs. The same danger arises if we become "too heavenly" and deny our human needs for security, relationship, and self-fulfillment in the earthly sphere. Trying to be "just spiritual" disembodies us and makes our humanness irrelevant.

Am I describing you? If so, be willing to take note and make a conscious decision to use discernment to make lifestyle choices that honor both halves of your nature. No one can restore balance to your life but you!

Recently during one of Eupsychia's two-week intensives, one of my students developed a severe ear infection. It was so aggressive that one side of her face swelled up and her temperature raged to 103. Because she was a spiritual healer with a strong belief in hands-on healing, she asked another healer in the group to work on her. But my staff intervened and insisted that she be taken to the emergency room at the nearest hospital first. She returned to the retreat center, loaded with antibiotics and pain medicine. When the medication began to take hold, she asked for and received the hands-on healing she believed in. Almost immediately, she felt better. Having honored both sides of her nature, conventional medicine and spiritual healing combined to work marvels.

As the mediator between the spiritual and earthly selves,

your human psyche, like Psyche of the myth, links Spirit with matter, soul with ego, and so keeps us on track toward full realization of both aspects of our being. When we follow the laws of our human nature, our spiritual life, too, unfolds with no distortion. Like a lake with no ripples, our human life reflects perfectly the heavenly light of higher truth.

LIFE LESSON

Resolving the Mystery of Dualism

If this Seed Thought is drawing your attention, it may be time for you to examine the assumptions about your nature that you learned as a child. As you go through your day, pay attention to the judgments you make about your own behavior. Are you harsh with yourself? Do you label certain thought patterns or actions as wrong or sinful? Do you punish yourself for "misbehaving," as if you were a naughty child, or reward yourself with treats for "being good"? Do you second-guess yourself, stifling your urges toward free expression or personal growth and label them as misguided or selfish?

Conversely, perhaps you have trouble remembering to think of others, and are prone to meet your own needs at someone else's expense. Do you have trouble keeping friends? Do people avoid you? Do you find that you seriously defend your need to be alone, when truly you are isolated? Perhaps it has never occurred to you that key relationships have a spiritual intent. A dead honest critique of your be-

havior may be called for, to help you shift to a more integrated way of being that can bring you much more
fulfillment.

Splitting off your spiritual urges from your human needs
does disservice to both aspects of your being. Spirit, soul,
and body are one—like vapor, water, and ice. There is no
separation. Learning to stand tall in both your earthly and
heavenly natures is the key to being centered and vitally alive
in this complex world.

It is human nature for the ego to want to be high and
holy. This drive toward transcendence is why so many people
get hooked on drugs, sex, passionate fighting, or other ways
of accelerating their physical energy. Our ego longs to fade
into the undifferentiated bliss from which we came into incarnation. Yet, at the same time, our soul wants to descend
into matter. It craves the earthly pleasures of sentient existence that our physical nature makes possible. This pull of
our dual aspects toward ascent and descent make up the
chorea mystica, or sacred dance of human life.

As both an ego and a soul, we can learn to live rhythmi-
cally within this tension. When the pull toward spirit is
strong, we must honor our natural need for quiet reflection,
making sure that we give appropriate time to cultivating the
inner life. Your daily spiritual practice does not need to be
tied to a particular religion; it can be your own internal process of honoring the soul and its journey, whether through
meditation, prayer, or other contemplative activities, or
through dance, music, immersion in nature, or creative expression.

When our energy is more outgoing, we can throw ourselves into physical activities, actively engaging in those tasks and enjoyments that give embodied life its savor. The pleasures of earthly existence—delicious food, passion and sexual activity, strong feelings, and freely expressing our creative urges are not rewards for good behavior. They are the natural means of expression for our physical being.

Staying conscious in both aspects of our being is the key to learning this life lesson. The only absolute on the soul's journey is that we *own* our own experiences, including our errors and imbalances, and not project them unconsciously onto others. When we practice awareness of everything we do, without intent to harm ourselves or others, we become authentically who we are intended to be, secure in the double vision of our human and divine nature.

As is stated in the ancient Hindu scripture the Upanishads: "To darkness are they doomed who worship only the body. And to greater darkness they who worship only the spirit. . . . They who worship both the body and the spirit, by the body overcome death, and by the spirit achieve immortality."*

*Quoted in John Conger, *Jung and Reich: The Body as Shadow* (Berkeley, CA: North Atlantic Books, 1988), p. 1.

Exercise

Imaging the Self You Were Born to Be

The inner mental picture we create of ourselves is not simply imagination or fantasy. Images have reality and soul power. The mental images we hold of our ideal self can help bridge the gap between the self we are today and the self we long to become.

Take a moment to sit quietly and reflect. In your mind's eye, picture yourself as you are right now—your physical self, your psychological and emotional self, where you see yourself to be on your soul's journey toward awakening.

Now see yourself in a situation in your current life—at work, at home, with your family or friends. See yourself dressed in your usual way, speaking and acting as you usually do. Allow this mental picture of yourself to become as vivid as possible. Feel your way into it, and notice what emotional responses arise. Ask yourself, How do I feel about the self I am right now?

Let this image fade.

Now, in your mind's eye, use your imagination to create a picture of the self you wish to be, your ideal self, the you that you hold up as perfect or complete. Be patient and give this image time to arise from your subconscious.

At first you may sense this image as a generalized essence . . . then as a vague "memory". . . . As the image becomes clearer, feel your way into it and notice how it is to inhabit this ideal you. Ask yourself, How do I feel about myself now? Is this the me that I was born to be?

Now allow your mind to hold both pictures . . . the you that is and the you that might be. Let the two images turn toward each other and slowly come together, as if a double image were coming into sharp focus.

Hold the joined image for as long as you can and sense its beauty and power! And see who you are in all your glory! Now stretch out your hands toward heaven, while your feet stay firmly planted on the ground. Notice that in this pose, you are a column that links your earthly self and your spiritual nature. Imagine that the column is now a conduit pipe through which the inspiration of Spirit is flowing into your body and your life.

As a final step, you may wish to describe your ideal self in your spiritual journal and note the intentions and emotions that arose for you during the exercise.

Seed Thought Two
The self is greater than its conditions.

The next step on the path of individuation is learning that the Divine in us, whether we call it self or soul, is our highest guide through any human predicament.

Like Psyche, we often experience ourselves as being at the mercy of the gods, impersonal forces that seem to shape our lives. Standing in the middle of our own picture, we are often incapable of self-reflection and may lack the ability to evaluate anything or make decisions. Whether our conditions manifest as a sense of our being born into the "wrong" family, or of lacking enough money or education to live the life we long for, or of having been married too young or to the wrong person, or of being "burdened" with a child or elderly parent with special needs, it's easier for us to blame circumstances for our limitations than it is to recognize that the self always has choices.

No matter how chained to the rock we feel ourselves to be, how enmeshed in circumstance or in overidentification with some larger-than-life ideal we fear we can never live up to, the divine spark within us steadily moves us toward our unfolding. Throughout the first part of her adventure, Psyche, we recall, seemed to be a pawn of enormous forces—the oracle of Apollo, the jealousy of Aphrodite, the immaturity of Eros, the guile of her human sisters. Yet despite all this, and unknown to her, the Divine Self within was moving her toward lighting the lamp of higher consciousness.

When the impetus for growth stirs within us, we often don't realize what is happening. Our drive for self-actualization can bypass the intellect completely. Without knowing that we have decided anything, we simply find ourselves saying or doing something we'd never intended, something that tears up our current plans and forces us to move on.

I remember a time that I'd made a firm decision to stay in a marriage, even though it had lost its magic. Dreading having to start over, I'd talked myself into believing I could stay. I had even made a resolute pronouncement to that effect to several friends in Baltimore as I boarded a plane to travel back home to Texas. During the flight, I read a book, not giving my decision a single thought. My husband met me at the airport as planned. To my utter surprise and horror, the first words out of my mouth were, "It's over with us. I love you, and I am leaving you." I remember thinking, "Who just took over my vocal chords?"

We can imagine Psyche asking herself a similar question when her impulsive act of disobedience led to her separation from Eros. Yet the impetus for growth coming from the Divine Self within cannot be denied. Years later, long since divorced, my former husband and I have come together again in a whole new way. Looking back, we can see that our separation had been part of a bigger plan for both our lives.

Getting caught up in life's predicaments and believing we *are* these conditions is the plight of every incarnating soul. Anytime you have that depressed feeling that something in your life is just not working, or you feel completely stuck, or consumed with self-doubt, know that you are letting some condition "get you." Stop right then, go within, and remind yourself that nothing external can destroy the immortal self, your embodied soul. As the Hindu Bhagavad Gita states:

Weapons cannot hurt the Self and fire can never burn him. Untouched is he by drenching waters, untouched is he by parching winds. Beyond the power of sword and fire, beyond the power of waters and winds, the Self is everlasting . . . ever One. Know that you are, and cease from sorrow.

Nothing "out there" can ever harm the divine essence of who you are. Only your shadow's reaction to it can. Anytime you need the courage to move beyond an entrapment, you can call on the Divine Self within. It will respond. It will remind you to name the condition, but then to step out of it. Naming a thing enables you to disidentify with it. The sense of distance that results helps you to see your problem objectively and to figure out how to resolve it.

As was true for Psyche, every human condition you pass through is a lesson in love. Life conditions are simply the chess board upon which all the pieces of your life are placed. You must have a playing field upon which you can bring your soul's life to earth. When you are unwilling to wake up, you get caught in a tape loop and repeat whatever lesson you've not yet learned. The names and geography may change, but until you bring its root cause to consciousness and take responsibility for clearing it, the issue will remain the same.

Your family or religious background may have trained you to seek definition in outer circumstances, to focus on external accomplishments and to view inner contemplation as a waste of time. This Seed Thought corrects this grave mistake. In order to come to consciousness, you must have the courage to disobey society's rules when you sense that they are not based in truth.

A wonderful story exemplifies that you are always much more than your current conditions. Years ago, my friend and colleague Ram Dass was talking on the call-in show he was hosting in New York. A woman caller was on the line, crying that she was desperate, that she was overdosing on drugs and was going to kill herself. She went on and on about how helpless she felt. All she wanted to do, she said, was to die. After listening for several minutes, Ram Dass replied calmly,

"Please put the one who dialed this number on the phone. It's her I want to speak with. She can save you."

Living with the Wound of the Heart

If this Seed Thought contains a lot of energy for you, you may be living in denial about some condition in which you are caught up that needs to change or to end. You may have lost touch with the bigger picture. Just reading these words may begin to shift you toward consciousness of the problem, which is always the first step in any process of growth.

Recognition is the key to integration. Often the simple act of bringing a condition to consciousness dissipates the energy that holds a problematic situation in place. When we can name the condition, we have stepped outside it, which means we are disidentifying from some knot of our own making. From this objective view, you will see that you are the self and not the condition at all. Once you've experienced this freedom, you can honestly own and accept your responsibility in whatever you got caught up in, and then you'll find that it no longer commands your attention. Bringing to light whatever old ways are holding you back from your highest expression and recognizing them for what they are is the first step toward releasing your limitations. This is your job description as a conscious psyche!

Once you come out of denial and disidentify with this problem you are facing, the next step of healing is to look at your situation from the highest point of view. Ask yourself, What is the soul lesson for me in this dilemma? What role am I being asked to play? From the soul's vantage point, you can dip down and enter into any fragment of your local life that's in trouble. Bringing your highest self into play allows both soul and ego to cooperate in your healing. You may see from above that you've allowed yourself to overidentify with one of the wounded fragments of your being. Taking the soul's perspective can help you bring this wounded part up and fill it with love, as a way of re-membering the divine dimension of who you are.

Another way to feel your way out of overidentification with your current problem is to remember that any set of circumstances in which you find yourself is not "just personal." Seen in its broadest context, any individual's problem belongs to everyone—in fact, to all of humanity. As you heal your own wounds, you heal some aspect of the general human condition. Anything you make conscious sheds a little more light on the psyche of humanity as a whole. For, at the highest level, we *are* all one. I remember wailing once, "Why me? Why me?" At that, my wise spiritual counselor replied, "Well, why *not* you?"

Of course, once you know and accept your true condition, you face another potential pitfall, the agonizing gap between the actual and the ideal, between where you are now and where you'd like to be. You may recognize a condition that needs to be transcended but still lack the conviction, the willingness, or the insight to make the necessary changes. However, from the soul's perspective, the anguish that you feel when you know that you are not living up to your full potential is your motivation to press onward. Without it, it's easy to give up and let fate or circumstances make your choices.

For instance, I know a man whose partner subtly encouraged his drinking problem because it kept her in control in their personal relationship and in the business they ran together. Whenever a disagreement came up, she would urge him to relax and have a drink, while she took care of everything. A health crisis finally made this man hit bottom. As he recovered from a serious operation, he began to notice how his illness empowered and energized his wife. He saw that he had allowed himself to play the part of a helpless child, "mothered" both by his addiction and by his passive cooperation in the ways his partner was using his addiction to control him. Coming to consciousness meant giving up being taken care of and making a lot of tough changes: getting professional help to combat his alcoholism, and ultimately, leaving both his business partnership and his marriage. Now, years later, sober and married to a healthy and supportive woman, this man looks back in disbelief at how thoroughly he had lost his true self in his conditions, believing all the while that he had no other choice.

When the promptings of the Higher Self call you to move on and you do not respond, quite often something disastrous happens to get your attention. In the physical sphere, for instance, you may know that it's time to clean up your diet, but you prolong your resistance until serious illness strikes.

Emotionally, you may get the message that you must quell your frequent angry outbursts. Arrogantly refuse to respond, and you risk damaging a precious relationship. Or mentally, you may be righteously holding on to some opinion that is now no longer viable. Resist the needed change, and you wind up feeling abandoned and misunderstood when intimate associates distance themselves from you.

When you begin to make changes to come to greater consciousness, you may find that you are grieving, or full of anxiety, or convinced that your life no longer has meaning. These feelings signal that some large cycle may have ended in your life, and that circumstances or even people that you've taken for granted are falling away as part of this change. Taking the soul's perspective allows you to rise above life's inevitable cycles and alterations. You may not need to let go of the things and people you love after all, though growth does require that you let go of your attachment to how it's always been. Whenever a new chapter opens in your life, you must let die what needs to die. Once you've brought your old accumulations to the surface, owned them, and let them go, you've done your job. Spirit will do the rest.

Exercise

Transcending Your Conditions

Here's a simple mental process that can help you remember the bigger picture in the midst of any uncomfortable circumstance you face. Taking a moment to focus inward will turn you in the right direction for Spirit to move you forward.

Find some private time to reflect on a current problem in your life, some condition that is giving you grief. Allow this situation really to come in on you—feel it, be fully in it, absorb its essential quality. . . .

Now, using your imagination, see yourself rising up and out of this scenario and viewing it from above. From this higher vantage point, look down and see what it is that's *really* going on. . . . What's the lesson or the deeper meaning? . . .

Remember that Psyche's divine purpose was to reunite beauty and love. Reflect on what *your* god or goddess function is and how it is to manifest in this situation. . . . What spiritual gift or talent do you bring to it? Take as long as you need to allow the answer to rise into consciousness. . . .

Now see the ego story that is keeping your conflict in place. . . . Ask yourself what attitude or idea you are holding on to that keeps this story going. Remind yourself that your life is a sacred journey and that conditions arise in order to help something good work itself out along your road. Reflect now on what positive quality you've been struggling to bring into your life. . . .

If you are feeling trapped, abandoned, insecure, hopeless, or melancholy, identify the feeling but do not attach to it. Let the feeling pass on by as though on ticker tape, with compassion for your ego self who is feeling all this. . . .

Now notice *who* in you is letting the feeling pass on by. This one is the Higher Self, the part of you who is beyond the drama. Identify with this one if you can . . . and see how this greater identity feels as it takes shape in you. . . .

From this higher perspective, see how it might feel to lighten up and stop taking your problem so personally. Imagine yourself as moving beyond your current melodrama, seeing your personal story as a scene in the play of humanity's healing. . . . Notice how your feelings start to settle down as you take on a wider perspective. . . .

Now listen to the inner silence for a while, and create the space for guidance concerning what you must do to just naturally start flowing in. Take as long as you need to get the message. . . .

When you feel finished, slowly allow yourself to come back to this reality. Reflect for a moment on this statement by Carl Jung: "What, on a lower level, had led to the wildest conflicts and to panicky outbursts of emotion, now looks like a storm in the valley seen from the mountain top. This does not mean that the storm is robbed of its reality, but instead of being in it, one is above it."*

Finally, take some time to draw or write about the process that just happened in your inner life.

Seed Thought Three
What you say "I am" to has a way of claiming you.

What you say you are, you become. As poet and therapist A. L. Kitselman wrote, "The words 'I am' are potent words.

*C. G. Jung, Collected Works, volume 13, *Alchemical Studies* (Princeton: Princeton U. Press/Bollingen, 1983).

Be careful what you hitch them to. The thing you're claiming has a way of reaching back and claiming you."*

The words "I am" carry the power of manifestation. When the God of Exodus spoke to Moses from the burning bush and gave him a message for the children of Israel, Moses asked, "Who shall I say has sent me?" In other words, "What is your name?" God's answer conveys a powerful truth. "Tell them 'I Am that I Am' has sent me to you."

Any spiritual psychology will agree that "I am" holds the essence of a person, which is divine—the self that is never sick or damaged, never even subject to birth or death. We must never say "I am" to anything less than this. Here's why: The Divine Self does not behave like a "thing" with a personified identity. It is an archetypal matrix only, an energy pattern that contains all the qualities of a completed human being. It's the "I" who will take the form of whatever we say "I am" to at any given time.

Many ways we commonly say "I am" are completely off the mark. The difficulties we experience, such as depression, alcoholism, or poor physical health, should be seen as conditions we have, or labels we've taken on, not as the essence of who we are. Unfortunately, the English language causes trouble here, with common expressions such as "I am depressed," "I am a cancer patient," "I am a food addict." When we define ourselves in this unconscious way, these statements become our way of knowing who we are.

*A. L. Kitselman, *E-Therapy* (New York: Institute of Integration, 1974), p. 1.

Try it for yourself. Take a moment and list in your mind all the limiting notions you hold about yourself: "I am a divorced woman." "I am the product of a broken home." "I am an alcoholic." Now language these conditions in a way that disidentifies the essential *you* from the problem: "I have a feeling of depression." "I have a cancer challenge." "I have difficulty controlling my drinking." See how much lighter you feel? How much more room you have to move? This way of speaking and thinking is much more accurate and in tune with the laws of the self.

Even positive roles such as "I am a success" can be a problem. All identifications create an expectation that we must then live up to. For instance, "I am an excellent mother" may work fine while your children are young. But once they're grown, overidentification with the motherly role can be problematic for all of you. You may feel you have no life except when you're performing a good-mother function. So remind yourself of what you learned in Seed Thought Two: You are not your conditions! You are not your current problem! Thinking that you are is a question of mistaken identity.

I once knew a prominent commercial realtor who was a well-respected community leader, a generous husband, and a dedicated father of two beautiful young daughters. On the surface it looked as if he had everything going for him. A shock rippled though our community when we heard that he'd shot himself. It seems that a business transaction had turned sour and threatened this man with financial ruin. His suicide note said that he'd failed his family and could not live with this fact. So many of his friends had made millions, he couldn't face being identified as the one who had failed. His wife and two little girls were devastated. They loved him for the husband, father, and caring person he was, not for the money he could earn. Yet because of his misplaced identity, he thought he was saving his family shame by bowing out.

We can all become lost in the conditions we pass through when we confuse them with our identities. At this stage of our individuation we begin to realize how our self-definition creates the lens through which we view life. It determines what we allow to upset us, what we focus on, and what we give priority to in our lives. As we travel the path of direct experience toward greater consciousness, we learn to say "I am not this; I am not that," until we come to acknowledge the Divine Self we are at the core.

The parts of us that can be so immature or destructive are called subpersonalities. Each carries the identity of a certain aspect of us that has a particular set of needs. A subpersonality is activated through a set of circumstances that stimulate a particular unconscious theme. Then, like clockwork, they have us act out in a predictable pattern of behavior. When a subpersonality overtakes you, your voice and demeanor change as you convert into this character you've become. A subpersonality might say, "I *always* feel this way when I'm around a male authority figure!" Or "This is how I *always* behave when a good-looking woman walks into the room." That word *always* is a dangerous bedfellow. As we come to consciousness, we realize that we are never *always* anything— except creative and divine!

how to use psyche's seeds

Here are some typical subpersonalities who can seize our identities. You may recognize some in yourself: the True Believer, the Southern Belle, the Perfect Son or Daughter, the Bookworm, the Don Juan, the Jock, the Control Freak. And, of course, the Alcoholic or Drug Addict. Every time we find ourselves living out such a label, we have the opportunity to recognize an important truth about ourselves. We can appreciate a subpersonality for showing us our weaknesses. But we mustn't ever give one power over our life, for these partial selves do not reflect the soul. They create the fog on our mirror only to point out to us what conditions we need to wipe clean.

Let me tell you about one of my troublesome subpersonalities. For years I had trouble being a mother who could calmly and confidently discipline her children. Having been raised as an only child by very permissive parents, I'd had little training that suited me for mothering three biological children plus three stepchildren. I would be too lenient, too much the big sister or best friend, then realize I was being taken advantage of. Resentment would build up until I flipped into the opposite mode. I would get the screaming meemies, threatening consequences I could never implement. "Go to your room, and don't ever come out again!" "I'm never feeding you another meal!" When I'd behave like this, one of my youthful charges, more mature than I, would humorously call me Mafia Mom, roll his eyes, and whisper to the others, "Just wait. She'll get over it." I finally had to learn to get over it and get real. With much inner work, and a boost of self-confidence, I learned to overcome my inexperience so that I could mother my children effectively.

When you discover you are hosting an unwanted subpersonality, it's wise to give it a name that makes plain its exaggerated antics. Naming a condition is halfway to healing it. Humorous nicknames that personify these characters reduce your shame. Then, when they pop out, the ego won't get hooked in having to defend itself.

But you have to be careful. Conditions like alcoholism, diseases like cancer or diabetes, or mental illness labels such as manic-depressive or obsessive-compulsive, can easily captivate your self-image. It's very easy innocently to say "I am" to these things. And though these categories of human behavior do have a reality that can sometimes guide you to an effective treatment, they are *not* who you are. Never forget this! It's the key to your ultimate healing from any one of these conditions.

Many people in addiction-recovery programs today are realizing they have outgrown the label "I am an alcoholic" as being their entire identity. The label served them for a time while they developed a stable sobriety. But at some point, the alcoholic identity becomes a skin too tight to contain the ever-expanding self. When, after twenty years of sobriety, a person says, "Hello, my name is John, and I am an alcoholic," it's probable that other aspects of this beautiful person are suffocating in that constricted identity.

How we identify ourselves and our world is much more the determiner of our experience than we realize. If I know

how to use psyche's seeds

I'm a soul passing through a lifetime and experience myself as such, I'm not as likely to be hurt if I fall short in a certain role or lose a limited identity. I'll still have a sense of self. Most suicides occur because of the "I am" statements we assign ourselves. The power of the word must be honored as we learn to redefine ourselves holistically.

But don't misunderstand me. Every limited identity has its place. While living within its boundaries, we are assimilating its lessons and gaining an experiential understanding of how that particular part of ourselves behaves and what it needs. This knowledge allows us to take responsibility to get the need met and then to die to it so we can move on. It is great wisdom to know that we are to relinquish, or disidentify with, what we've outgrown. Identification, in Buddhist terms, is attachment; disidentification is nonattachment. We must learn to be good at both and to know when each is appropriate.

Psyche's entire journey could be viewed as a search for her true identity. Your psyche's journey has the same goal. Like Psyche during her first task, we "sort the seeds" as we go along, learning to discriminate between the me and the not-me, the essentials and the nonessentials, through the process of identification and disidentification.

We each have the potential to wake up one day and know that *we are all of it*. As consciousness itself, the human psyche is designed to live always at its own growing edge. We take on. We let go. We take on. We let go. Until, at last, we fill in the entire blueprint. In this manner, moment by moment, we make conscious our own process of be-coming.

And then, when we're at home with our Highest Self, we can relax and just be.

Letting Go of Attachment

To progress on our spiritual journey, we need to descend into physical life and ascend back to the Source, over and over again, as if moving in a figure eight. As we do, the divine soul and human personality work together to weave us into the wholeness of our full becoming.

We saw this pattern in the Psyche myth in the contrast between Psyche, representing the embodied soul, and Eros, representing the abstract principle of love. While Psyche got "down and dirty" struggling to complete her human homework, her other half, Eros, remained above it all, hidden away in the celestial realm of the gods.

These same two tendencies can manifest in you, sometimes in extreme ways. Do you get overly involved in personal dramas? Do you have trouble letting go of something or someone even though you know it's over? Are you obsessively concerned with material possessions or accomplishments? If so, you may be more like Psyche at the beginning of her journey.

Or, on the other hand, do you detach too easily? Are you hesitant to make a commitment or to allow yourself to get involved in life's ambiguous conditions? Do you tend to be unfeeling and removed? If so, you may have taken the young Eros as your guide.

Each side of this sacred equation has its benefits and pit-falls. Some of us are better at involving, or identifying. We know how to dive in deeply and experience life. We are capable of intimacy and do not avoid feeling states. This way of living can be very fulfilling, but it has its drawbacks. We can get trapped in some dreadful melodramas or obsessive emotional preoccupations and not know how to get free. Living in drama can become an addiction. When that happens, we don't feel alive unless some crisis is going on. If we run out of personal dramas, we even take on others' problems as if they were our own! If this is your lesson, you may feel as if you're caught in an endless string of crises, unable to distinguish between what belongs to you and what you should allow to pass by.

Others of us may be better at disidentifying, at knowing how to rise up and out of any condition. If this is your pattern, you may have learned this skill through training in a spiritual path that focuses on equanimity and transcendence. But it also may be true that you wish to avoid intimacy or any demands on your feelings. Rather than engaging, your tendency is to withdraw emotionally when things get sticky. As we learned in Seed Thought Two, viewing a situation from a lofty vantage point can be helpful in recognizing the soul lesson hidden in a human predicament. But in order to resolve a problem or heal a human wound, you have to come down to earth and be willing to get your hands dirty!

Some of us may get caught in distancing ourselves because we've made the mistake of trying to move too quickly beyond a situation that we've not fully integrated or thoroughly understood. Our withdrawal may indicate that we lack the courage or conviction to face the hard parts of life, or to work through unfinished business with someone from the past. If this is your story, the lesson may continue to return until you get it. Remember, your unhealed issues can show up at a board meeting just as easily as they can in a private family squabble.

The key to balancing your tendencies toward excessive involvement or withdrawal is to watch yourself and see what attracts your emotional energy—what you think about, talk about, and allow to occupy your time. As the Psyche myth taught us, neither extreme involvement nor extreme withdrawal can take us to the wholeness we seek. In order for the human Psyche to ascend to goddess stature, the divine Eros must descend from his heavenly refuge and come to her aid.

So do a little self-examination now and see where you fall on this continuum. Get in touch with any tendencies to which you are attached that you may have outgrown. Once recognized and owned, your unconscious attachments begin to dissipate, and the extremes in your life come more into balance.

Some growth is, perhaps, required of you now. Think about it. Are you ready to change? If so, the following exercise may help.

how to use psyche's seeds

Exercise
Disidentification

Your attachment, whether it is to a physical habit, a long-held emotional pattern, some limited or outmoded idea or belief, or a certain person, may stand in the way of the clarity that you seek or of some new and higher self-definition. If you are ready to let go of this limitation, here's what to do:

First, observe the attachment. Name it specifically. Remember to language your tendency correctly. "I have an attachment to" rather than "I am."

Then, in your mind, watch yourself letting go of whatever it is that you're holding on to. Even if you feel you can't let it go just yet, use your creative imagination to see yourself behaving as though you have.

Mental practice makes perfect! How do you see yourself dealing with this situation beyond your attachment to it? Make it up. Then write it down and concretize this new way. Now you must practice being that one who lives on the other side of this roadblock. Imagine it as vividly as you can.

Often some old, outworn attachment can be released mentally, even though it may take some time for your physical life to reflect this change. But you don't have to wait until then to resolve this issue from inside. Stay conscious and use your Observer Self to notice how you're doing with the issue. Be willing to be patient and let the process take hold.

Finally, remind yourself who you are in your highest essence, the Divine Self or soul that is beyond all dualism and is always perfectly in balance.

Here's a summary of this simple process. Write it down and use it as a daily affirmation for several days or weeks. Practiced with focused intention, this exercise will release you.

Step 1. Observation: "I have an attachment to . . ."
Step 2. Disidentification: "But I am not . . ."
Step 3. Reidentification: "I am pure consciousness and the impulse to act as my Highest Self."

If you have worked diligently through these first three Seed Thoughts, you'll find that your first chakra has come into balance. Your physical consciousness and instincts are more refined. You have a strong will to live and the ability to bring order into your daily routines through right action. Your fears and feelings of isolation have begun to dissipate, and you are grounded in many practical ways. Your soul has firmly taken up residence in your physical body.

Now we'll enter the next phase of the journey of transformation, the balancing of the emotional body.

Seed Thought Four
**The human shadow is not evil;
it has a sacred function.**

To balance our emotional nature, we first must face the human shadow and acknowledge its sacred function. The shadow, you remember, is the dark, unknown side of our personality—the qualities and tendencies we are ashamed of and deny having, even to ourselves, because they threaten our ego's notion of who we are. These uncomfortable parts of our nature must be met, accepted, understood, and integrated before we can move ahead on our sacred journey.

The shadow that hides behind our public facade has an embarrassing tendency to reveal itself in actions beyond the ego's control. The more we try to push the shadow down, the more powerfully it takes over and acts out the parts of the psyche we have been denying. As an aspect of the emotional body, the shadow often shows up as a clutched feeling that makes us want to scream, run, control, lie, or hide. When the shadow is activated, we may feel hypersensitive and reactive, experience uncontrolled explosions of feeling, or behave in ways that lead to humiliation. We can all empathize with the politician whose speeches about upholding the public trust are undercut by revelations of financial impropriety, or the fire-and-brimstone preacher who is arrested in a vice raid. The shadow is nothing if not democratic, and some time or another, we have all been caught with our pants down!

In the Psyche myth, we saw the role of the shadow enacted by Psyche's jealous sisters. When they voiced their "suspicions" that Psyche's unseen husband was a terrible monster who would soon devour her, Psyche was receptive to their words because they echoed her own repressed doubts and fears. Thus it's fair to say that it was the unacknowledged shadow of Psyche's love for Eros that set the entire story in motion. Sounding a wake-up call to inner work is the shadow's sacred purpose. It forces us to work out the kinks in our psyche and won't leave us alone until we accept and integrate the darker side of our nature.

The shadow can act out in subtle ways as well. When your reaction to another person manifests as an extreme of either attraction or repulsion, it may be that you perceive in this person some aspect of your shadow. Here are some clues that you may be responding emotionally to a projected piece of your unacknowledged self:

- You perceive someone as an enemy and yourself as a victim.
- You perceive someone as a savior or as a paragon of truth and authority and believe that this person holds the key to your salvation.
- You become obsessed with someone else's problems and set about to "do" this person's life.
- You fall madly in love with someone who is not available or appropriate.
- You sacrifice all your money, time, and energy to some cause that you decide is more important than your own life.

Do any of these sound familiar? If so, you probably have shadow work to do! Projecting a piece of the shadow onto another person and then falling in love with this secret mirror image is more common than you might think. I have heard so many men and women complain that they always fall in love with the wrong person, or that everyone they get serious about turns out to be no good, often in similar ways.

Why this happens is no mystery. Until the hidden material in our psyche is brought to consciousness, we get tricked into working with our unacknowledged parts in our external life, often by making the same flawed romantic choice again and again.

But there's another way the shadow comes into play in our relationships. A woman's ideal inner masculine, an unrealized aspect of herself, is known in Jungian psychology as the *animus*. A man's inner, unrealized ideal feminine is his *anima*. Until you understand that you're working with these psychic characters as inner processes, you'll project these ideals onto your romantic partner. You'll expect your human partner to become this contrasexual "other" for you, not realizing that what you're really seeking is a part of your own self that you've been unwilling to own. As we saw in Psyche's story, it takes a lot of hard, inner work to resolve confusion about this "other half" with whom we so long to mate. As we become conscious of the masculine/feminine aspects of the self, we can see that our error is trying to make a human partner measure up to a high archetypal ideal!

All romantic relationships tend to mix earthly and spiritual desires. We long for that perfection of the poets' dreams—perfect because it never has to manifest—while simultaneously we want the passion of a real human partnership. If we seek spiritual communion at the expense of earthly desires, we risk becoming ungrounded, filled with illusory expectations that are impossible to fulfill. We become "so heavenly, we ain't no earthly good," as the country-and-western lyric humorously puts it. If we ignore our spiritual needs and stoop too low to fulfill our desire for passion, we risk playing out the role of some shadowy archetypal character—a Don Juan or a femme fatale who lures us into seductive fantasies that threaten our responsible engagement in family and community life.

Once you bring to consciousness and integrate your projections, your love life moves out of the shadows. You'll discover, as the Psyche story taught us, that your deepest love affair is always with the inner Beloved, the soul. No matter who your earthly partner is, the key to success in any relationship is the marriage of your inner psyche and eros—your human qualities and your inner divinity. The human shadow's sacred function is to bring to light everything we wish to hide and deny about ourselves, especially our unexamined illusions about love. As we recognize and accept all that we are, the shadow integrates and heals.

The shadow is not all negative traits, however. The unexpressed side of your nature contains both desirable and undesirable elements—talents, needs, and skills that yearn to be owned and expressed in order for your life's purpose to be fulfilled. Your lover self, your playful self, your priest or priestess self, your leader self, your artist self—any of these can be part of the shadow. When you deny your shadow qualities, you tend to project these elements onto other people in your life. You idolize a friend who is an artist, for instance, rather than developing your own latent artistic talent. Or you react with intense criticism born of jealousy when you come into contact with a person whose position of leadership mirrors your natural gifts as a leader or your own unacknowledged drive for power.

These unexpressed aspects of the self are energetic and always find a way to make themselves known. The key is staying conscious. Consciousness disempowers the shadow; it can only act out when we are in the dark. When the shadow is exposed, we can zap it with our compassion and understanding. Made conscious, the shadow can no longer turn on us behind our backs.

Sometimes revealing the shadow requires an act of supreme courage. I remember a process we did in one of Eupsychia's healing intensives. Participants in what we called a shadow dance were to dress up in costumes that represented an aspect of their shadow they were ready to own and heal. One beautiful young woman with a history of acting out sexually when she was drunk showed up in a G-string and very little else. At first, we were all shocked. Our emotional response to her uninhibited display of sexuality reminds me of Psyche's fear of the rambunctious cavorting of the powerful, masculine rams of the sun she faced in her second task. Some of my male staff members felt they needed to leave, and wives were grabbing their husbands in possessive, fearful ways. All of our sexual shadows were activated.

Then the music came on, and this woman began to walk around the room, looking each of us in the eye. Fortunately, we all fell into our hearts. We honored this revealed aspect of her, bowed to it, and gave her nothing to feel shame about. This process of acknowledgment went on for several minutes. I feel tears coming to my eyes as I recall the woman's brave self-disclosure in our process group the next morning. She said that she felt that our acceptance had healed this immature, uncivilized part of her that had almost ruined her life. As Psyche did when she used her womanly wiles to approach the rams and gather their fleece without disturbing them, the feminine principles of love and patience can help us tame and integrate the shadow, even when it takes its most overt and terrifying form.

Facing the shadow is an essential step along any spiritual journey. Look into the biography of any well-known spiritual leader. You'll find that most engaged in some kind of personal shadow dance at some point in their careers. Pretending to be high and holy all the time is itself a form the shadow can take. People who tell you they have no shadow are standing in it as they speak! Denying the shadow is a dangerous avoidance of our humanness that takes us into a cul-de-sac of unconscious behavior that blocks our growth.

Shadow work is how we become tempered and honed, as a masterful potter works with clay, matching it to an inner image until its true form emerges. As an aspect of our Higher Self, the human shadow creates the fire by friction that opens up the unconscious mind and exposes to the light of consciousness whatever needs to be pared away. So have a little compassion for your shadow, who is crying out to be accepted and invited to walk along with you. When you realize that the shadow is that part of you who has the toughest assignment, your heart will open to this unloved part of yourself.

Remember, whatever is unconscious has power over you; it can burst out and hurt or surprise you or others in unintended ways. But whatever you make conscious, you have power over, to use as a quality or skill that helps make you whole. You mustn't fear making your shadow conscious. And you must realize that the greater self within you will always rule over these wounded, fragmented selves. As Jesus said in the Gospel According to Thomas: "If you bring forth what is within you, what you bring forth will save you. If you do not bring forth what is within you, what you do not bring forth will destroy you."

LIFE LESSON

Embracing Your Shadow Side

If you feel split between loving and hating parts of yourself, shadow work may be the lesson that is up for you right now. Ask yourself: Do I put myself or others down when they behave in ways I don't approve of? Am I afraid of revealing my true feelings in some situations? Am I arrogant? Impatient? Always trying to be too perfect? Do I gossip or get a secret thrill out of seeing others fail? What kinds of people cause me to overreact in negative or positive ways?

Also explore how your shadow may be affecting your relationship life. Are you perpetually dissatisfied with your partner, while you nurse a secret fantasy that somewhere out there is your soul mate or twin flame? Or do your relationships all seem to fail in the same way or for similar reasons? Remember, until you love yourself, you can never really love another, or even have empathy for what another person wants or needs. Only you can meet your need for love. No one, not even an intimate life partner, can do this work for you.

Regardless of the ways your shadow is manifesting, the first step in dealing with it is to lighten up and be a little kinder to yourself. This in itself helps to integrate the shadow, though deep shadow healing often requires depth therapy. If you catch yourself overreacting to a person or situation, here are some ways to defuse your shadow's reactivity and come back into balance:

- Bring to consciousness what is causing your reaction and claim the issue as your own, even if a part of you still believes it's the other's fault.
- Discharge the pent-up feelings appropriately, by talking to a reliable therapist or a well-balanced friend. Or express your feelings privately, through tears, an angry journal entry, or a vigorous workout at the gym.
- Transform the energy that remains into some positive expression. Throw yourself into your work, write a poem, draw, paint, or garden madly.

Whatever you do to acknowledge the shadow, also remember that by revealing our disowned or hidden parts, the shadow is serving a sacred function in helping to move us toward wholeness. As we bring more of ourselves to consciousness, our passion for life is enhanced and we begin to feel more authentic and alive. Moreover, owning the shadow is the basis for forgiveness and compassion. Since every human being casts a shadow, recognizing our own heals our self-righteousness and opens our hearts to a loving appreciation of the common humanity we share.

Exercise
Shadow Play

Bring to mind some part of yourself you simply cannot stand. Perhaps you have a temper, or love to gossip, or use your sexuality in some manipulative way.

If you have trouble identifying a shadow trait, remember that your shadow lives in your emotional body. So take some time to reflect on the last time you overreacted to something or someone. Ask yourself: What did that situation or person remind me of about myself that makes me uncomfortable?

Once you've identified some shadowy part you'd like to work on, close your eyes and go within, and visualize the image that comes to mind when you think of this particular negative self. Now invite it out. See it as a character who lives inside you. . . . Notice how it's dressed . . . and what age it is. Watch it move around and notice how it carries itself. . . . Which of your qualities does this image hold for you?

Now begin a dialogue with this shadow self. Ask it how long it's been with you. . . . Let it tell you what it's protecting, and how it came to be. . . . Merge with this part of yourself and be this shadow self for a moment or two. Are painful feelings coming up? If so, go into the essence of the pain and discover its root. Perhaps some old childhood wound . . . maybe someone or a part of yourself you still need to forgive. . . . Whatever feelings arise, let them "bleed out." Do not repress them. . . . This expression is part of your healing.

Now, with an open heart, tell your shadow that you accept it, and watch what happens inwardly. . . . Tell your shadow that you are inviting it to walk alongside you in life, remembering, of course, that You are the one in charge. As your shadow self comes closer to you now, love it as much as you can from wherever you are in your visualization. Then watch what happens in your mind's eye. Take as long as you need for this part of the process. . . .

Once you feel some integration taking place, allow these inner images to become as gray mist, until you are once again aware that you're back in this reality.

Finally, take some time to process this experience. It's wise to write about or draw an image of your shadow to help you make it real.

Seed Thought Five
Victimhood is a false concept that makes you powerless.

Victimhood is an insidious and powerful part of the personal shadow—so powerful that it can overtake your entire life. Victim consciousness is spawned from a grave misunderstanding about who you are. The true self is an empowered self, never anyone's victim or pawn. It never occurs to the empowered self to blame anyone else for anything!

how to use psyche's seeds

Psyche, as we saw, began her sacred journey feeling that she was a victim of the gods. Not until she successfully completed her second task did she begin to realize that she had her own skills and power—in fact, that she had some claim on divinity herself. To awaken to this stage of unfolding is a massive leap in consciousness. Such knowledge removes any feeling of being tossed about by the hands of fate. It brings us face-to-face with our cocreative responsibilities for making our life what we want it to be. The purpose of this Seed Thought is to help awaken you to this realization.

The most obvious manifestation of victim consciousness is a tendency to blame someone or something for whatever aspect of your life is not working well. You may believe, for instance, that your current problems are the result of your upbringing or of mistakes your parents made. Or you may blame an early life trauma, such as an experience of sexual abuse, for all of your current misery.

Though it's a hard lesson, the spiritual wisdom of the world teaches us that nothing that ever happens to us is an accident. Nor is any event of our life "just personal." Everything that we experience serves a sacred purpose for our life and for humanity as a whole. Even our birth into a particular family where harmful abuse occurred is part of the sacred design for our soul's purification and transformation.

This statement may make you angry or bring up a sense of divine betrayal. "Why," you might be thinking, "do innocent children have to go through any kind of abuse? Where is the sacred justice in that?" You're forgetting that babies and small children are big souls in little bodies, and that the strongest, most mature souls are often asked to take on the hardest lessons. Questions about why we suffer are among life's most difficult mysteries. They have plagued seekers of spiritual truth the world over. Most spiritual paths agree, however, that there is a reason, though we may never know it, why each soul carries the cross that it bears.

It's quite difficult sometimes to accept that darkness must be experienced before it can be transformed and that whatever each of us goes through in life is our part in the divine scheme. If we could know all the mysteries of karma and other cosmic laws, we'd fully understand. But we come into incarnation blinded by an innocent willingness to enter into the human condition—blinded on purpose so we'll do our work. Among the most transformative lessons we learn as we grow toward spiritual maturity is that there are no victims, even in what appear to be the most heinous atrocities of life.

Victim consciousness is based on our ignorance of three fundamental truths:

- that all our suffering has a sacred purpose;
- that though we cannot avoid suffering, we do have the power to control how we respond to life's misfortunes; and
- that all lessons in life are lessons in love.

Let's look at each of these truths, for they are essential to progress on our spiritual journey.

The sacred purpose of suffering is to help us transform

and grow. Anytime we think we are a victim of anyone or anything, we've forgotten that we always draw to ourselves exactly what we need—not necessarily what we want, but what our soul knows is right for us to experience. For instance, when a betrayal or relationship failure tears up some part of your life, you can generally look back and see the part you played in setting up the circumstances. Perhaps you idolized the person in a way no one could ever live up to. Or perhaps you allowed someone to idolize you! If so, you helped sow the seeds of your own betrayal.

Whatever form suffering is taking in your life right now, ask yourself what you did to cocreate this particular story line. If your suffering is manifesting as a lack of financial resources, ask yourself how generous you have been to others—and to yourself. Assess honestly how willing you've been to learn to make and to manage money. If you are suffering from loneliness, ask whether you have been a good companion to yourself, as well as to others. If your suffering has manifested as physical illness, examine whether your condition has come about to teach you to revalue what's important in life. It's really this simple: the universe always says yes to whatever we call to us and turns it into our reality. No one can escape the great law of cause and effect.

Though we cannot avoid suffering, we can learn to respond to it with compassion for those who have caused us to suffer, and for ourselves. Forgiving those who have harmed us is one of the most healing aspects of Divine Love. When we forgive someone, we necessarily diminish our ego by relinquishing some pattern of self-righteousness. Our greater self knows that letting go of blame, including self-blame, is essential if the soul is to move us along on our sacred journey.

I remember a particularly poignant demonstration in one of our workshops of how we set up victim consciousness and how awareness of our pattern can help us move beyond it. A man in the workshop was given to playing the part of the wounded child. When it came time to do a process requiring a partner, he made it plain that he had to work with someone who would not "abandon" him. He went on and on about this. The woman who volunteered for the role was a very kind and caring person. The man felt relieved and lay down to do the meditation with closed eyes while his partner served as his protector. During the whole two-hour process, this woman stood watch over the man's space with a deep sense of commitment. Far into the process, she scooted away for one minute to put a blanket over another participant. At just that moment, the man sat up straight, opened his eyes, and yelled, "See! I told you this would happen!"

Later in the process group, the man was able to see what had happened. His expectation of being abandoned had called this exact experience to him. He saw that his life pattern was to set himself up to be a victim so that he could play out again and again his childhood story of emotional abandonment by his abusive parents. Bringing the pattern to consciousness was a major breakthrough for this man and the first step in healing his lifelong suffering.

As a therapist, I have seen how people use victim consciousness as a way of controlling others. These "victims" rule their families with their "weakness"—a stance that is much more powerful than confronting others directly. Professional victims have learned to use guilt to coerce others into doing what they want.

It's like the old joke about the adult son who telephones his elderly mother in Florida.

"How are you, Mother?" the son asks.

"Not so good," the mother replies.

"What's wrong?" the son asks with concern.

"I haven't eaten in seventeen days."

"Seventeen days!" the son replies. "Why not? What's wrong?"

"I didn't want my mouth to be full when you finally called."

If you have a perpetual victim in your family, it's hard not to fall into the trap of thinking that it's your responsibility to save this person. This is not love; it's codependence, and it holds the pattern of victimhood firmly in place.

You can build whatever reality you want, not by changing your outer circumstances or anything that's already been set in motion but by carefully constructing the mental image of where you'd like to go from here and who you'd like to be. Just as you can call to you experiences of suffering, so, too, you can define your future. If you feel that a wound from the past is holding you back, reframe whatever terrible thing happened to you as a "fortunate fall"—an opening through which something wondrous entered your life. Ask yourself what gift of greater understanding or deeper knowing resulted from this pain? You may be surprised at the answer! If you honor your past for the good it's given you, you can stop wasting your precious energy by looking back, and step confidently ahead into the future.

Victim consciousness keeps you focused on the "enemy out there," on someone who owes you something. This view disempowers you and sets up the conditions for you to suffer again and again. As long as you expect yourself to be a victim, a string of perpetrators will stretch far into your future life, as far as you can let yourself think. Ironically, it's your thinking that creates them! Whatever you obsess about and feed emotion into will manifest in some form. You really are this powerful. It's much more fulfilling to empower your spiritual self and to take on responsibility for cocreating your own future.

Victim, Scapegoat, Enemy, Orphan, Betrayer—all these self-created roles bring us archetypal labors of love to help awaken us to our true identity. Direct experience can teach us that the Divine Self is greater than any one of these. It's very true that this world is an unsafe place. This life we live, with all its delights, is shot through with ambiguity, loss, and vulnerability. No one is immune to life processes, which bring both pleasure and pain. When we overcome our victim consciousness, we begin to reconnect with our true purpose for being here and to what we've come here to heal. This deep commitment allows us to live our life to the fullest. We no longer see fate or other people as having power over us. We start to cooperate in the divine plan for us and to focus on our part in its unfolding.

Ruling with a Scepter, Not a Sword

A sword cuts things in two: "It's me against you." A scepter symbolizes the quiet rule of the centered self: "You and I are one." The empowered self holds a scepter, not a sword, for it knows that everything is connected.

Scepters or wands stand for the spiritual or creative dimension of consciousness. Wave a magic wand, and you can change the picture in a flash. Unlike the hero who rules with a sword, the heroine wins over opposition through love and creativity. Our world is starving for this gentler ruling style.

Go within for a moment and reflect on your own style of rulership. Do you create change in your life with a sword or a scepter? If you generally wield a sword, you may wish to ask yourself whether this harshness is doing more harm than good.

Or perhaps you feel right now as if you are powerless and lack the will or the ability to make positive changes in your life. If this is your state of mind, you may have become your own oppressor. The sword of self-denial is keeping you down more effectively than any external enemy or circumstance. To rule with a scepter rather than the sword, you must give yourself permission to be exactly where you are right now, even feeling yourself to be a victim, if that is your truth. You can only begin to change from where you stand at any given moment. To move to the next level, you must first accept yourself as you are. Anything else is a lie.

Even if you've made some horrible mistake or have taken a wrong turn, see if you can be gentle with yourself while owning your part in the predicament. Try to recognize some new talent or positive quality you've been incubating that you hadn't yet noticed you possess. This new talent may be the very one you're being asked to birth now from your focus on this Seed Thought.

I had a client who named his empowered self Viking King. In his imagination, he designed this new part of himself to act just the way he thought a Viking king would, and practiced the role whenever he felt the need. One morning he approached his intimidating boss with this new personality and reclaimed his power in the relation-ship. The picture between them changed for good, just as if my client had waved a magic wand. The two even became golf buddies.

The following exercise may help you step beyond victim consciousness into a new reality.

Exercise

Reclaiming Your Freedom of Thought

When you are trapped in victim consciousness, you feel yourself to be at the mercy of someone or something. "What's the use of fighting it?" you say. "I can't win in this situation. Or if I do, something will come along and ruin it anyway."

If this is your pattern of thinking, take some time to get in touch fully with the feeling that results. Remind yourself of times or situations in which you've allowed yourself to feel victimized and how uncomfortable it is to lose your sense of control over your own thoughts and actions. Don't feel guilty about having caused yourself to suffer in this way. We all play the victim sometimes. Laying a guilt trip on yourself is just another form of victimhood.

Though it's true that you may not be able to change what's taking place in your outward circumstances, you never need to feel that you are powerless. The magic can happen in your very own mind. If you are ready to move beyond victim consciousness, here's what to do:

Call up in your imagination a time when you really played the victim part to the hilt. See this pitiful self plainly . . . and give this part of yourself a name—a humorous one, perhaps, like Pitiful Polly or Wilting Willie.

Now, with all your heart, call up a feeling of forgiveness for this pitiful fragment of your personality. . . . Forgive it for the limitations it has held you to. . . . Remind yourself that whatever happens to you served a sacred purpose. Tell yourself that you no longer need this kind of limitation, and release this partial self now, with love. . . .

Imagine, if it seems appropriate, that you are taking this unloved and unloving part of yourself into your arms and enfolding it into your heart. . . . As you do, note the you who is embracing this part of yourself, for this empowered one is who you truly are!

Take some time to reflect on the fact that no matter what happens to you "out there," you have the freedom to reframe the situation and to move in a new direction, right now. You can make a decision to act in a new way. See in your mind's eye the part of you who can behave in this self-empowered fashion. . . .

Be sure to anchor this new self in your consciousness as the one you truly can be. Let it take shape in your mind and focus on it. Watch how it stands, how it's dressed, how it behaves. Remember, you are creating a new aspect of yourself to help move toward a more integrated way of being.

Remember also, you are the meaning maker of your life. Only you can decide the meaning of anything that happens. What's more, you create your own future by what you set up now, so invent a daily practice that you can commit to until this new aspect or identity becomes so natural that you don't even have to think about it.

Seed Thought Six
**Your desire nature is God's Love
manifesting in your life.**

The next challenge in balancing the emotions is learning to make right use of your powerful capacity for desire. This is one of the hardest psychospiritual truths for us to assimilate because of our religious imprinting. Many of us have been taught to fear human desires and to repress them as shameful or less than spiritual. It's certainly true that strong feelings can be chaotic and overwhelming. When you're captured by some huge desire, you may feel yourself to be out of control or you can get frightened by the intensity of your attractions. But you have to remember that your passions provide the fuel that moves you forward toward your own unfolding. In fact, seen rightly, all of your magnetic attractions, even sexual passion, are manifestations of Divine Love. One of your most important tasks on the sacred journey is learning to trust that your desires are how God's love translates into a human heart. Every desire is a reminder of something you need in order to be whole, even though what you might need may be a very tough lesson. Otherwise you wouldn't feel the pull so acutely.

What is it, do you suppose, that draws you strongly toward another human being? It's certainly not the mind. You know very well that it's impossible to talk yourself into loving or desiring someone, no matter how logical or perfect the pairing seems to be. Rather, attractions tend to come upon us like fate, beyond the control of ego or intellect. If you think back over your own personal love stories, you'll probably discern that each contained a necessary lesson or soul expression that needed to manifest in your life. Letting your deepest desires guide you is not self-indulgence. You can trust that the true desires of your heart are a push that comes straight from the Source.

Spiritual psychology tells us that the desire to merge with something or someone is an expression of the sacred craving to merge with Something or Someone greater than ourselves. A soul desire always leads you to a better place and never causes harm to you or to anyone else. The compulsions and addictions of a needy ego, on the other hand, can give us valuable information about our unmet needs, but we may be required to discipline the ways we allow ourselves to act them out. Feeling a strong desire and refusing to deny it does not mean you have to act it out. No matter whether a desire arises from the soul or from the ego, discounting or repressing it is never appropriate psychologically. A repressed desire simply goes underground into the unconscious, biding time until it bursts out in some self-destructive or harmful way.

The key, of course, is learning to discriminate between soul desires and the compulsions or addictions of a needy ego. A sacred desire feels like an intense, almost unbearable longing to be someone greater—to be more, to be home, to be completely fulfilled. You may actually feel this desire as an aching emptiness in your chest in the area of your heart chakra. An ego desire, on the other hand, feels more like a clutching in your stomach or solar plexus. It manifests as an urgent feeling that makes you jumpy. You want to do something right now. You feel pushed toward some compulsion, with little thought of the consequences. People who have suffered from addictions know this place as "wanting what I want when I want it." Sugar binges, sexual acting out, and physical violence are examples of uncontrollable urges that reflect imbalances in our physical or emotional body. Since acting on such desires harms us and others, they clearly arise from the ego and not from the soul. Yet even in these negative cases, I believe that the soul is at work. Every desire or intense craving, even a harmful one, can point toward some area of personal work that you haven't yet mastered and must deal with in order to be whole.

Your psyche is not seeking perfection; she is seeking completion! Trying to stamp out your natural desires just makes more and more of the very thing you're trying to get rid of.

It is your responsibility to make sure you get your basic needs met in ways that never harm yourself or another. If you are ashamed of your desires or pretend to be above them, you are in danger of being overtaken by any denied feelings of anger, jealousy, victimhood, or other shadowy emotions.

I once had a client who was so ashamed of his compulsive sexual behavior that he was in therapy with me for months before he told me about it. Then one day he confessed that though he had a wonderful committed mate, he was slipping out late at night and going to an adult bookstore to have sex with strangers. This compulsion was a complete mystery to him.

I listened to his tale with quiet concern. Rather than reacting with judgment, I said to him, "Well, since everyone involved is a consenting adult, why don't you just enjoy what you're doing rather than feeling ashamed of it?"

The man nearly fainted. He couldn't believe that I didn't regard him as some kind of pervert. So I said it again, this time more strongly: "If you're going to act this way, do it and dig it! But there's one qualification. You must stay absolutely conscious the entire time you're engaging in this activity, moment by moment, feeling by feeling. Make your late-night excursions a mindfulness meditation, staying completely present and aware during the entire experience."

A few weeks later, the man came into my office chuckling with delight. After he had indulged in his compulsion three more times, it died completely. The first time he'd watched himself enjoying all the sensations without shame. The next time, much of the pleasure was gone, and he just watched himself engaging in this activity with a certain puzzlement. The third time, the whole scene just got funnier and funnier. The more clearly he saw what he was doing, the more he laughed. He couldn't even stay involved. He told me that he went home that night feeling deep gratitude for his mate and much reverence for the whole process of conscious sexuality. Shortly after this, my client left therapy and moved away. When I saw him about two years later, he told me the compulsion had never returned.

This method of working with addictive behaviors is tricky, but it is sometimes very effective. It is based on the idea that any action carried to its extreme will flip over to its opposite. This approach can sometimes help overeaters. I encourage them to fill their refrigerators with every food they crave, all available to them around the clock. However, they must commit to staying conscious of every bite as it goes into their mouths and of every feeling they have while eating.

Being fully present is the key to the healing. When we indulge in a desire that feels shameful, we don't stay in our bodies while we act it out. Instead we look the other way so we won't have to face whatever it is that we're doing. Binge eaters who consume a quart of ice cream while engrossed in a television program are typical of this pattern. Because we are "not there" while engaging in the experience, the ego convinces itself it is always starving for whatever it craves. When the psyche is allowed to fill itself up to satiation with what it desires, however, and we remain fully present in the body to enjoy the sensation, we cannot forget that we have fulfilled a desire or pretend that we have not done whatever we are ashamed of.

I've witnessed this same process dozens of times in my workshops, where breathwork is used as a modality. When a person is trying to escape from an intense negative memory that's surfacing as a result of the breathing practice, my staff and I move in and say, "Stay with it. Exaggerate the feeling. Give it full intention!" Our task is to give the person much loving therapeutic support while the repressed memory and its attendant feelings are allowed to come to the surface. When an emotion arises, if it is allowed to express itself fully, it will release. The process takes only a few minutes. When we allow our feelings to come to the surface, rather than denying them or pushing them down, a sense of calm washes over us, and our heart space and throat feel warm and open. Release is the way the emotional body heals.

Unfortunately, many of us have been taught the opposite. We've been shamed into believing that desires are sinful and that we must never allow our strong feelings to show. So we pretend that everything's fine—even to ourselves—and live on the surface of our lives like plastic people. Think of Psyche in the myth blithely describing her married life to her visiting sisters, and you'll see an example of this behavior. Because Psyche could not admit her night-world passion for Eros, even to herself, she made herself especially vulnerable to her sisters' jealous schemes. Repressing our desires and denying our feelings is never the soul's path to wholeness. When they are not acknowledged or expressed, desires and other strong feelings can create emotional blocks in the body-mind that lead us ultimately to grief.

Interestingly, the twinned psyche knows two ways to work through past issues and purify your desire nature: through symptom and through symbol. When the psyche seeks to heal itself through symptom, it projects its concerns onto the relationships in your external life. An inner issue with authority, for instance, may be mirrored in heated conflicts with your boss, your parent, or your spiritual teacher. As you work through these external conflicts and heal the outer relationships, your inner issues resolve as well. This is the ego's way of healing you.

The symbolic way, on the other hand, works from the inside out. Through visualization, self-reflection, meditation, breathwork, journaling, psychotherapy, and other interior processes, you come to understand the image behind the issue that's manifesting in your outer life. When you take full responsibility for your inner dynamics, you learn to handle your problems from the inside. As a result, the outer behavior that expresses the problem changes. For instance, a woman whose binge eating is rooted in a desire to be loved works on learning to love herself, and her addiction resolves. This is the soul's way of healing you.

The more you can "act in," the less you need to act out. Committing to the path of inner work saves you from the problems that arise when you project your unmet needs onto others. When we're unable to acknowledge or express an unfilled inner need, we often blame other people or life in general for denying us what we desire. Though projections can certainly be powerful teachers, inner work through the symbolic realities of myth, dreamwork, and visioning can reveal the symbolic meaning of the unhealed parts of the psyche so that they can be addressed at their psychic root without the melodramas often caused by projection. The work we have been doing with the Psyche myth is based on this inner path to healing.

Doing personal work that heals your past creates a transparency for your whole self to shine through. Once you've brought to consciousness the shadowy desires and other strong feelings that you've been taught to repress, your inner mirror will be shined up. Then you can trust that your desire nature will express your highest ideals. You can follow your bliss with confidence, because you won't be drawn to actions that harm others or yourself.

Only learn to acknowledge and release, completely and honestly, what is bothering you, and you will no longer need to look back. You'll develop the free attention to move forward into new and higher ways of being. Once something is finished, it's divinely forgotten. It no longer saps your precious psychic energy. Jesus knew this. His final words were these: "It is finished."

LIFE LESSON

Honoring the Divinity of Human Love

If you've tuned into this Seed Thought, your desire nature may be asking to be fully exposed so that you can move beyond its shadowy inauthentic side and allow its sacred beauty to bloom. Perhaps the time has come for you to clear some unacknowledged or repressed desire that's been standing in your way, maybe for a long time. Remember, there is no desire in you that is harmful to hold if you mix the ingredients of self-love, harmlessness, and wisdom into its expression.

To heal your desire nature through inner work, here are the stages you need to work through:

- The symbol or symptom appears.
- You recognize and name it.
- You enter fully into the desire and feel it all the way through.
- You accept what is happening by giving your experience a sacred meaning.
- You forgive yourself and release the hold of your desire by giving it to the Divine.
- You stay conscious and aware as your compulsion or engagement starts to fade.
- Your desire nature is transformed and purified.

The mystical Christian tradition and many other spiritual paths acknowledge that our human and divine natures are one. They know that there is a human part of us that dances its way into life through desire and its fulfillment and a spiritual part that remains pure and whole no matter what our human self experiences.

When you trust the divine Source of all desire, it's easier

to see what a need you feel is trying to reveal. You can then decide whether it is appropriate for you to act on your desire, or whether compassion for yourself and for others demands that you sacrifice the need to act and instead use the desire as a subject for the work of inner transformation. If you know a desire to be destructive, be willing to stay conscious with it until it reveals its mystery. When you see through to the real need buried underneath the desire, you'll discover that it's nothing to be ashamed of. Most often, you'll find that the need is for more acceptance or more love.

Would you really want to live in a world devoid of passion and the intense search for satisfaction? The saddest people I know are those who withhold themselves from living, afraid they might violate some spiritual law if they allow themselves to enjoy this human life. Your heart and the Heart of the Divine are one. The heart's wisdom comes to you through feelings of being attracted or in love. You can trust your heart never to lie to you. It will tell you that when you love some-one or something intensely, you are being called to dance.

Exercise
Invoking Eros

Eros, the beautiful god of love and inspiration, rekindles the spiritual fires of our passion for living. Eros makes possible a constant revival of the soul. When we feel ourselves to be in love—with some activity, some person, or just with life itself—we are vibrantly alive and connected to the Source.

Eros is a living spirit in your psyche. You can always access him through your creative imagination. If your vital fires need to be rekindled, or your energy and zest for living need to be restored, the following exercise can help you call him in:

Close your eyes and see what Eros looks like as he appears inside your mind. . . . Let the energies of this inner beloved penetrate your heart and fill your entire body with divine feelings of love. . . .

Now let these divine feeling express themselves in a very human way as you reflect on someone in your life that you cherish now or have loved very deeply at some time in the past. . . . Allow your imagination to play over every feeling, every memory, every physical sensation connected with this loved person so that you really experience this remembered love. . . .

Now allow these loving feelings to roam outward into the world, toward a favorite place in nature . . . a small child . . . a cherished animal. . . . Let your feelings of love pour over anything that arises on the inner screen of your awareness. . . .

Now allow your imagination to carry you to some project you are currently undertaking . . . some artistic creation . . . or cherished plan. . . . As you think of this project, give it focused attention until you feel a warm rush of love and inspiration coursing throughout your body . . . and bless your project with this same warm and tender love. . . .

In this loving space, allow Eros to be revealed to you once more. . . . Now he is bending close to you . . . now he is whispering a message into your ear. . . .

Thank the god for his message of inspiration and slowly allow yourself to return to your ordinary reality.

Take some time to reflect on any message you may have received and to write about it in your journal. Know that in communing with Eros or any other inner partner, you have found, as Carl Jung wrote, "a relationship that seems like the happiness of a secret love, or like a hidden springtime when the green seed sprouts from the barren earth, holding out the promise of future harvests."*

These last three Seed Thoughts have focused on healing the emotional body. As you studied them, you developed a strong will to feel and the courage to allow creative, energetic forces to move through you without fear. As your second chakra comes into balance, your sexuality and relationships seem less extreme and more centered. You have learned to deal rightly with pleasure and passion. Right feeling is the integration of Psyche's second task.

In the next three Seed Thoughts, we'll move up the ladder of wholeness into the sphere of the centered mind and open heart.

*C. G. Jung, Collected Works, volume 14, *Adam and Eve* (Princeton: Princeton U. Press/Bollingen Press, 1970), p. 432.

Seed Thought Seven
**We learn to live within the tension of
opposites as walkers in two worlds.**

The light and dark sides of your nature, as you can now see, both emanate from one human-Divine Self. The light is your conscious psyche, all that you have already made known. The dark is your unconscious psyche, all that is still unknown, unexpressed, or denied. Both sides contain a sacred truth. In fact, you could say that one could not exist without the other. As Carl Jung observed: "The One seeks to hold to its one-and-alone existence while the Other ever strives to be another opposed to the One. The One will not let go of the Other because, if it did, it would lose its character; and the Other pushes itself away from the One in order to exist at all. Thus there arises a tension of opposites between the One and the Other."* Perhaps you have felt this opposition within yourself and not understood its sacred and eternal nature.

The shadowy and luminous sides of the self are mirrored by the dark and light aspects of the world you inhabit. To progress on the spiritual journey, you must face the divine ordeal of knowing just how to relate to both sides of human life. Your position is perilous. Like Psyche standing on the banks of the river Styx as she faced her third task, you may feel yourself to be in danger of being swept away by the dark and suffering aspects of human life—war, hunger, disease,

*C. G. Jung, Collected Works, volume 11, *Psychology and Religion* p. 119.

human misery. If you lose your footing, you risk falling into the darkness of depression and loss of meaning.

Your task as you face the world of darkness is to stand tall in your true identity as a light bearer, one who is willing to meet the dark on its own terms, matching its strength. When you stand in your personal truth despite the darkness that threatens to engulf you, you embody the spiritual self who holds steady in the tension of opposites, as all true spiritual warriors do. Living within the tension of opposites requires that you find the zero point in the middle where the energetic pull from both extremes is balanced. This balance is as necessary internally—as you struggle to harmonize the shadowy and light aspects of your human nature—as it is when you face the oppositions and polarities of the external world. Standing at nil, the point at which the magnetic pull of the two contrary poles of existence is in balance, you are able to think and to act clearly, without overreacting to either extreme. From here, you act rather than react.

Though the tug of war of duality confronts you in many aspects of internal and external life, let's consider how it affects the balance between the masculine and feminine aspects of existence. Whether you're a man or a woman, you've internalized a set of culturally inherited assumptions that have influenced your being on every level. The ultimate duality is good versus evil, which in the spiritual sphere often translates into heaven versus earth and, unfortunately, into masculine versus feminine. For five thousand years at least, the world's recorded spiritual philosophies have held that whatever is light, heavenly, and male is good, and whatever is dark, earthly, and female is evil. Though the resurgence of devotion to the Feminine Face of God has, in recent years, tried to redress this horribly mistaken belief, the damage done by years of oppression of the feminine principle cannot quickly be undone. In truth, of course, we are all—both women and men—earthy creatures who get our feet dirty while traveling down the middle of life's path. The light of Spirit shines through you everywhere you go, even in the dirt, because your very essence *is* light.

The tension of opposites between the masculine and feminine aspects of existence manifests both internally and in our worldly relationships. Psyche, you recall, had to develop her unacknowledged inner masculine qualities and bring them into balance with her inner feminine side before she was ready to reunite with her lover Eros. For you too, as you've learned, the dark only becomes terrible when you fear to know it.

To own some dark or hidden aspect of yourself doesn't mean you have to act it out. It means that you acknowledge the contrary feelings or desires as a part of you and take responsibility for having them. If you resist knowing both sides, you may swing back and forth like a pendulum, caught in the grips of unconscious and opposing drives such that no transcendence is possible. For instance, you may be willing to own your prim and proper side but resist the pull of the side of you who wishes to be wild and zany. That wild and zany part does not disappear just because you fail to honor it. What happens, as you know very well, is that your wildness bursts out at an inappropriate time or else it catches you up in harsh judgments of someone's else's wild behavior, since you are unwilling to acknowledge your own.

Standing in the tension of opposites requires that you understand and accept that the Divine has two faces and that, to be whole, the self must honor both. As Jung explained, "God unfolds in the world in the form of paired opposites, such as heaven/earth, day/night, male/female. . . . The Self is a complex of opposites precisely because there can be no reality without polarity."*

How might this necessary complexity of opposites manifest in your life? In your work life, your passion (the dark) and your spiritual purpose (the light) can join to become an impassioned vocation—what the Buddha called right livelihood. In your relationship life, sexuality (the dark) and spiritual love (the light) can raise your lovemaking to the level of worship—you and your partner joining together as god and goddess. Appetite (the dark) and delicious food (the light) can make a meal a feast for the senses and a spiritual offering to the god within. Anger and grief (the dark) in a singer's voice (the light) can turn a song into a celebration of heartfelt passion and the triumph of human nature over adversity. You must always remember that both aspects of your nature have something precious to give you. When the Divine connects with physical form in balance and harmony, Beauty and Love—Psyche and Eros—are made visible.

Understanding the tension of opposites can also help heal

*C. G. Jung, Collected Works, volume 11, *Answer to Job*, p. 369.

your external relationship. I remember a recent conversation with three of my women friends, all of whom are married to strong, overtly masculine mates. We were discussing the problems we were having communicating with our partners across the gender divide. Taking a clue from myth, we reminded each other that the heroine wins her battles by befriending the dragon, not by killing him. We four made a pact to put this advice into practice in our lives by consciously conveying the message that we loved and accepted our partners just as they are, shadows and all, instead of constantly trying to change them, as women are so prone to do.

Two of us sent our partners loving messages by E-mail just to say how much we loved them, and received immediate and warm responses. Two others used the telephone to communicate warmth and acceptance and achieved the same positive outcome. We're smiling now at the magic that's been unleashed in every one of these relationships. One of the men, who was always too busy to call his partner, is now calling her several times a day. The other three men have made clear that they appreciate the support we are giving them and that they consider us to be perfect partners. Riding the dragon is so much more fun than warring over who has control of the beast! This is a lesson that both men and women might usefully learn.

When you're confronted with a manifestation of the shadow and the light, whether within yourself or between you and another person, you have a choice of how to react. Fight it, and you risk losing everything. Acknowledge the opposition, even lightheartedly "kiss it on the cheek" to let it know that it's been seen, and you can go about your business in a higher, more loving manner. When you choose not to battle the fragmented parts of yourself or to oppose them when they show up reflected in another person, your true self is reinstated as master of its house. As was true for Psyche, your individuation can only proceed when you are willing fearlessly to face the dark and when the masculine and feminine within you and around you stand alongside each another in respectful harmony.

Anything that splits in two within your psyche signals that something is in the cooker—undergoing the process of transformation. Twoness is an intermediate state, never a final outcome. Opposites are always seeking to unite. Your job here on earth is to hasten this joining. As you practice being a walker in two worlds, you bridge the gap between One and the Other to create a pathway for the self to enter and take you to the new and higher way.

L I F E L E S S O N

Living in Two Worlds

As a walker in two worlds, you never try to escape into the higher regions of Spirit and shirk your responsibilities here. Nor do you allow yourself to drown in the morass of the material world. You take responsibility for all that you've taken on, and you never avoid serving others in meaningful ways when you encounter them along your path. Since you know your own nature to be both dark and light, your compassionate heart is always open to the struggles of others.

You walk in the overlap between the worlds, drawing first from the heavenly realm and then from the earthly. You are always in the process of breathing in and breathing out. When in-breath times are upon you, the inner spiritual life prevails; when you're out-breathing, you feel the urge to put something into concrete action in the material world. Now that you've embarked on a path of spiritual discernment, you'll recognize when each mode of being is appropriate.

The key to this Seed Thought is keeping your balance so that you avoid being caught up in one side or the other of the Spirit-matter polarity. You may be spending too much time on material concerns and ignoring the needs of Spirit. Or you may be so immersed in your spiritual life that you are neglecting the more mundane but essential aspects of life.

If this rings true for you, take a moment to think about what may be going on. Do you shortchange the world of the Spirit because it brings up old fears or unhappy memories of the religion of your childhood? Or have you been taught that it's selfish to place too much focus on the inner life? If you are ignoring the material side of life while you put all of your energy into personal growth or spiritual practice, are others having to take responsibility for your earthly obligations? Have you lost yourself so thoroughly in the inner life that you have become ungrounded?

The opposites within us never forget the One from which they sprang and to which they long to return: my passionate, spontaneous self and my dry, controlling intellect; my trust and my mistrust; my calm side and my excitable side; my ego's need to be a material success and my soul's higher calling. These opposites are magnetically attracted to one another like lovers pleading to relate. When you recognize these dualities as belonging together, you'll begin to feel more comfortable in your own skin, more at home in your doubleness.

You'll feel even more comfortable with the contraries you contain if you remember that every apparently negative quality carries a hidden gift. Look underneath your anger, for instance, and you'll find that you've been misusing the energy of enthusiasm or passion. Greed can clue you to something out there that you need to fill in some deficiency. If you're jealous of a quality you see in someone else, you probably have the need or the capacity to develop that quality yourself. Look for the transcendent quality in everything, high or low, and you'll find the magical sacred buried in the ordinary all around you. Try it. You'll see.

It's wonderful to realize that you never have to deny any part of yourself to be spiritual. You only have to be willing to be conscious at all times of what's appropriate and when. What's more, you have the capacity to stand tall in your centered self, whatever contrary winds swirl around you. The exercise that follows can teach you how.

Exercise

Standing at the Nil Point

This magical exercise can change your life. It will keep you at the zero point safely balanced between all contrary opposites, living as your Higher Self.

Find a quiet place where you can be alone for a while. Let your body relax and your mind settle down. Close your eyes and envision that you're standing in the center of a circle. You are that point in the middle of the circle. Stand there, tall in all your potency as a soul in human form . . . and anchor this feeling by envisioning it clearly and intensely for a moment. . . .

Now imagine that an invisible line of force is coming from the edge of the circle behind you, moving through you, and extending out in front of you to the other edge of the circle. As you feel yourself to be anchored there in the center, realize that nothing you have experienced in your life so far and nothing coming toward you in the future can move you off-center. Nothing on the time line of your life can have any effect upon your centered self. Take a few moments to recognize how this feels. . . .

Now imagine that a second line of force is coming toward you from the left edge of the circle, moving through you at the center, and extending to the circle's right edge. Recognize that no imbalance can knock you sideways and move you off-center. You are awake and present as a centering force, standing in the light of your own soul.

Now with your imagination, allow the circle to grow into

a sphere that encloses you completely. The sphere extends far above your head and way down into the earth below your feet. You can create this sphere of protection anytime you wish. The image can open around you like an umbrella anytime you feel yourself getting drawn into some kind of struggle, when you need to feel safe from some unwanted energy, or even when an imbalance from your inner life is threatening to overpower you.

Know that as you stand within your sphere of protection, anchored by the lines of force that hold you firmly in the center, everything that can upset your state of equilibrium has been excluded. You are held safe in a realm of pure consciousness, free of all contaminating influences.

Anytime you fall into a judgment or an attachment, you can return to the nil point by becoming still and using your imagination to create this circle of safety to stand within. I even use this visualization to create a zone of centered calm in chaotic airport crowds! From this central position, you are a conscious cocreator, completely in charge of your own destiny.

Practice this meditation daily for a while. It can help you remain centered no matter what is going on around you. It can also protect you from influences you were never intended to absorb. Those of you who are energy sensitives will find this technique especially useful. From nil, you can decide to detach or absorb the influences of the world at will.

Standing at nil is not a passive stance. The center point

between any pair of opposites contains the energy of both sides of the polarity. When you stand at nil, you live from the center, embodying your true essence.

Seed Thought Eight
There can be no outer experts on a path of self-knowledge; the learning comes from within.

One of Psyche's most important realizations was that every helper she encountered as she struggled to complete her tasks was an unacknowledged aspect of herself. The same is true for you. Everything that appears around you has a reflection in the inner world of your psyche. Once you understand how this marvelous mirroring works, whatever you meet can give your personal growth a powerful push.

The world around you is alive with symbols and synchronicities, potent images and powerful lessons, all of which can teach you something about the fullness of who you are and help you advance along your sacred journey. Yet there can be no outside experts on the path of self-knowledge. We come to understand the nature of our authentic self through our own experience, not by how someone else sees or defines us. We learn by studying the deeper meaning of the people, things, and experiences of this world. Once you commit yourself to a path of self-unfolding, the world becomes a giant classroom full of lessons that your soul will help you understand. Wise guides you meet along the way will direct you to your own inner wisdom. All guidance must be verified by personal inquiry.

how to use psyche's seeds

We learn the truth about who we are in mysterious ways, through flashes of color or light, through stories we read or see or hear, and through scenes and images that burst upon our consciousness pregnant with meaning. An acquaintance tells you a story about a stranger that strikingly parallels your own, and you suddenly remember a missing piece of your story. A bird flies across the evening sky at the precise moment when you need to be reminded of your own ability to soar. The color of a flower or a scent in the air triggers a memory that fills in a gap in your current understanding. As in the movies, a scrap of paper dancing in the wind becomes a transcendent symbol of beauty that pulls you out of some current despair. Sometimes the message is kinesthetic; goose bumps or a sudden headache jolt you into paying close attention to something you encounter. When you wake up to all the ways your soul is seeking to teach you who you are, every ordinary person and event in your life takes on special meaning. "Why did this just happen?" you ask. "What is the meaning of this?"

A symbol is a link between the world of Spirit and the world of matter, a messenger from the higher dimension that activates the psyche. It uses something familiar in the ordinary world to carry a deeper meaning than you can know with your intellect alone. Because the personal self is linked to the Greater Self at the heart of all things, you have the innate ability to view the world from a transcendent perspective. The centered self within you can gain access to this higher way of knowing by making the effort to read the symbols, metaphors, and signs everywhere around you in the world of meaning, and by seeing the deep spiritual root of everything you do. With your awakening powers of visualization, whenever you feel the need to use the power of image and symbol to resolve a conflict, you can look inside and find the images you need. Here's one way you might proceed:

Imagine that your inner consciousness is an upward-pointing triangle. The bottom corners represent duality, the yes and the no, or the two opposing sides of any difficult decision or conflict. The point at the top of the triangle contains the energies of the two lower corners plus something more that emanates from Divine Mind, to which it points. Now assign an image or symbol to each of the two lower corners. Hold the two images in your mind, and, as you inwardly watch them, see what image appears spontaneously at the top of the triangle. This symbol represents the synthesis you are seeking.

I once worked in a therapy group with a woman who had had several casual love affairs, though she claimed to be happily married. Then, one day, she discovered that her husband was engaged in a casual affair of his own, and she was filled with conflicting feelings of love and hate, rage and shame. I asked her to imagine a triangle such as the one I have described. At the bottom left corner, she was to image her husband's unfaithfulness. What came to her mind, she told me, was a strutting rooster! Opposing this image, in the lower right corner of the triangle, she was to envision a symbol of her husband's faithful and devoted love for her. The image that came to her was a pious minister, standing by her side. Then I asked her to imagine that the two images had joined together at the top of the triangle. The symbol her psyche placed there was the god of love, Eros himself, in all his sexy glory! The image of Eros helped this woman realize that there was a wild part of her that was turned on by her husband's indiscretions. It also helped her understand that her rage at her husband was a projection of her anger at herself over her own unfaithfulness. With these insights as a guide, she began working toward her own healing and the healing of her relationship.

Now, don't panic if you feel you have no experience working with images or interpreting symbols. Just making the commitment to intensive inner work—whether it's through journaling, meditation, group or individual therapy, self-help workshops or seminars, or dream interpretation—will get you started on the path. I've found that you rarely need a professional to help you understand your inner images when they appear. The experience of relating to these symbols is itself the teacher. Spend just a few moments with them, and the images and symbols of your inner life will teach you what they mean. Dream dictionaries, books that provide lists of symbols and their meanings, or other sources of formal instruction can even get in the way of your developing a fresh understanding of your own unique imaging style.

Just as Psyche modeled for us, we learn best through the circumstances that life presents. All soul growth takes place along the path of direct experience. As you continue to awaken, you'll see quite clearly that it's your inner life that determines your outer conditions—not the other way around! Unfortunately, you've probably been trained, as we all have, to believe just the opposite. We've been taught to seek truth from society's collective mind and to look to those who are considered to be experts for our answers. Consequently, we've given others the right to tell us what's good for us and how we must behave to be healthy or good.

Take the issue of a healthy diet as one obvious example. Pay attention to the health report on the morning news shows for a little while, and you'll see how confused and confusing the so-called experts are. One diet tells you to eat plenty of whole grains and complex carbohydrates. Another warns that you must strictly limit your carbohydrates and eat meat and eggs instead. We've let the lords of materialism, who thrive on public opinion, tell us what we should or should not eat, what possessions will make us happy, and even what we should look for in a partner or mate. The result is that too many of us are obsessively focused on the outer life, while our inner life is ignored.

It is certainly intelligent to seek sound professional advice from well-trained specialists at times. Many have knowledge we won't ever school ourselves to know. They can make suggestions, even give us diagnoses, but once we hear their opinions, we must take the responsibility for our own healing and well-being and follow the course to wholeness that we deem to be our truth. We're each so uniquely designed, there's hardly anything in life we can call consensual reality. Until the self within us strengthens, we are at the mercy of these outer authorities, just as Psyche was at the mercy of the gods. Waking up means discovering your own formula for right living.

Your Higher Self is more like an artist than a scientist. It is not looking for proof of its existence; it just wants to express itself through you. Remembering that you are part of the Divine frees you from the sense of powerlessness in the face of hard trials and difficult decisions. You enter into your own creation story with confidence and shift your focus from outer distractions to painting the beautiful portrait of the self realizing its own potential. The world is within you as much as you are within the world. This hybrid way of being is your birthright. You are your own most important teacher, and the self that you create is your gift to humanity's unfolding.

LIFE LESSON

Committing to the Life You Were Born to Live

You may have been looking in the wrong direction—to some outer expert—for solutions to your problems, when the answer is within you, just waiting for you to recognize it. The fact that you are reading this book suggests that you have realized that you must follow an inward track to the truth of your being and are willing to learn to trust this inner way.

Remember, the world around you is a mirrored reflection of your inner reality. Anytime you need to, you can reach out into the Big Mind of the world and take from it what your individual mind needs to understand. So take note of this as you walk through your days, moment by moment, making decisions. When you trust the inner life, you become a scientist of the soul. You document your findings by keeping a spiritual journal, recording all that you receive that seems important and noting how the messages provided by the world affect you. At first you may discount what happens as simple coincidence, but after a little personal research, you'll see that the revelations that come to you through coincidence are recognitions that the divine plan for humanity is being unfolded through you, as it is through all men and women who are willing to become conscious cocreators.

Perhaps this particular Seed Thought is speaking to you right now. If so, you are being called to take back your power as a self-actualizing person and to realize that you are capable of bringing to life your own special gift. You may be about to overcome a sense of personal inertia by taking a stand and getting busy with the task at hand. Just acting as if you already know that you have a role to play in the world's unfolding can jump-start a process of personal transformation. The people in your life will validate this process by telling you that you've changed, become stronger, lighter, more alive.

Stop a moment and ask yourself if there are any people to whom you have given away your power, any experts whose views you have adopted without question. Whose life or wisdom do you believe is more valuable than your own? It may be one of your intimate relations, or perhaps a doctor, a minister, or a psychic. Be willing to examine any dogma or formula you may have adopted that did not come from within yourself. Remind yourself that you are capable of free thought, of fresh thinking beyond what any authority in your life has ever told you is your truth. No one lives inside your skin but you!

The key to this life lesson is learning to live by the wisdom that tracks with your own direct experience. You have a "truth detector" inside you. It resides in your heart. Your heart will tell you when you are in the presence of authenticity, and it will warn you when you have strayed from your path or fallen into falsehood. Look inside, to the light that shines within, for there is the truth of the life you were born to live.

Exercise

Standing in Your Soul's Own Light

Imagine yourself to be standing in a circle of light, facing toward your future. . . . Note how it feels to be encompassed in this light. Let the light penetrate your mind and heart and flood all the cells of your body. . . . Now realize that this light is coming from the very center of you, from the realized self within. . . .

Notice how rich and full you feel as you stand there bathed in the light of your own soul. . . . In this state of consciousness, you need nothing from outside. You are complete. Realize that you already and always are this light. . . . As you come to know this light better and take responsibility for being it, the light that you are will expand further. Being a lightbearer for the world means that you live your truth and tell your truth through your loving heart. . . .

You can carry this image with you now, always, everywhere you go. No one has to know you're doing it. This is a private matter. As you make this process conscious, you'll begin to notice that you can gentle down any negative circumstance you may encounter. When light enters the scene, all darkness or negativity just naturally begins to move toward the center until it rises into combination with what is good, true, and beautiful, as in the visualization of the triangle. When you bring your light into any situation of conflict, the darkness begins to dissipate and people around you are affected, though they may not even know it.

You really are this powerful, if you allow the light of your soul to shine through.

Seed Thought Nine
An open heart is the bridge to the Divine.

The heart chakra, located in the center of the chest at the region of the physical heart, links our body and spirit and drives the life force that gives us our emotional and physical strength. Intuitively we know how important the heart is, not just to the physical body but to the energy that fuels the soul and personality. When athletes go all out to win, we say that they put their hearts into the game. When we are devastated by a tragedy, we say that we are heartsick or brokenhearted. When we are moved by a benefactor's generosity and compassion, we describe that person as being all heart.

Expressions such as these point to a deep truth that becomes more and more clear to us as we awaken spiritually. The emotional energy of the heart chakra is a bridge that links us to those higher realms where Divine Love continuously spins creation into being. When our hearts are open, we are filled with creative energy and connected to the pure power of the Source.

As the bridge between the human personality and the energy of the soul, an open heart helps us to heal the split between what is happening in our individual life and the Divine Plan of which all human lives are a part. An open heart is able to hold the tension of the opposites between what is and its deeper and more universal meaning. We know when we have bridged this gap because we experience a peaceful feeling of warmth and release in the center of the chest.

For example, say that you're brokenhearted over the impending loss of a loved one who is dying. You feel your grief as a hollowness or emptiness in your chest cavity. However, when you open your heart to a feeling of compassion for your loved one's suffering, and then to compassion for all people everywhere who are dying in pain, any brokenhearted emptiness you may feel is held in balance by a feeling of joy for the release from suffering that death brings. Similarly, a feeling of intense anger at a friend's betrayal can be held in balance by an openhearted recognition of your gratitude at the lesson you've learned as a result of this experience. We hold on. We release. Fullness and emptiness combine and balance. In the heart, pain and pleasure become one.

Mystics describe this divine tension as a state of bliss in which the whole self is engaged. As our sorrows and our joys mix together, the human personality contracts to the smallness of individual pain and expands to encompass the suffering of the universe. Pain and joy are neither wallowed in nor sought after; neither despised nor ignored. The personal and the collective combine and rise to the top of the triangle, into that third and higher synthesis, which is emotional wholeness and freedom.

The heart will always unite while the intellect tends to divide. Heart feeling is the opposite of cool, removed rationality. When we drop the mask of separateness and speak to another person heart to heart, our common bond overrides any sense of me and mine and links us as fellow travelers on the human journey. When we come from the heart, we just naturally allow genuine dialogue to take place and ground us in the absolute truth of the moment. An atmosphere of unconditional love encourages agreement and gentle change so that everybody wins.

Recently, in a family therapy session, I worked with a father and his teenaged daughter. The daughter had been caught after school smoking marijuana, and the father was so upset with her, he could hardly sit in his chair. The argument escalated as the father shouted his convictions about drugs and the stupidity of kids who use them. The daughter matched his level of distress, shouting back at him about how rigid and moralistic he was not to give her a chance to explain or apologize. The two were so entangled in their rage, I couldn't get a word in edgewise.

Then, suddenly, the father looked into his daughter's eyes, and the energy in the room shifted. His voice choked with tears, he took his daughter's hand, and said, "I'm not sure I know how to be a good father. I'm just so afraid that I'm going to lose you!" When she heard this heartfelt confession, the daughter's defiance just melted. In this communion of the heart, the two fell into stillness and then calmly began working out a plan for resolving their conflict.

Because the heart links our personal experiences of pain, loss, fear, remorse, and grief with the higher or spiritual meaning of human tragedy, it enables us to move beyond any self-centered reactivity. When our hearts are open, we can respond to another's pain with true empathy, experiencing both personal compassion and transpersonal objectivity. Both responses happen at once. Such expansion into the spiritual dimension is the cosmic purpose of personal suffering.

Heartwork is a universal process known as "initiation." The word *initiation* means "to enter into." Simply understood, experiences of initiation move us up the ladder toward becoming more fully realized human beings. Like Psyche, we can choose how we respond when life's troubles provide us with the challenges of initiation. We can close down and contract into a stance of self-absorbed grief or angry projection and blame. Or we can struggle to hold the tension between our personal feelings and the larger meaning of what is happening to us.

Like Psyche, we have a mission to fulfill. Our task is to prepare ourselves so that the Divine can flow through our human incarnation and out into the larger world. The process of initiation allows us to enter into a state of grace in which we are available to the deeper meaning of whatever we encounter. Initiates never fear the cycle of death and rebirth. They are always open to new feelings, new ideas, and new paths. Surrendering to the Divine within and allowing Spirit to guide their lives is their natural way of being.

The key to experiencing life as initiation is holding the heart open. A closed heart walls you off from access to the higher dimensions in which the creative imagination, inspiration, and intuition can be accessed. Shaken by the fear of change and death, you peer with vacant eyes at a threatening world full of uncried tears, repressed anger, and unexpressed caring. Spirit's flow can be impeded by repressed feelings that close the heart.

The open heart, on the other hand, allows life experiences to work their transformative magic. With an open heart, you think as God thinks and feel as God feels. An open heart is expansive and free. You stride fearlessly through whatever life presents. Spirit blows through you, and you see in your mind images of your new life, new possibilities beyond your current limitations. Seeing life through the eyes of the soul, you become an agent of inspired ideas and free thought. No longer burdened by heavy judgment and the world's opinions, you become transparent to creative becoming.

Coming from the Heart

When you live from the heart, you can relax and just be yourself. You have no ax to grind, no position to defend, nothing to hide. Coming from the heart melts your negativity and collapses all one-sided judgments, fanatical beliefs, and any need to be acknowledged as right.

A heart that is contracted around anger or resentment toward someone eats up your precious energy. You release anger and resentment for your own sake. "But," you say, "she really did abuse me. She doesn't deserve to be forgiven!" This way of thinking about people who have harmed you contains a flaw: your forgiveness never releases anyone from the dues they owe the universe for their unskillful actions. Karmic debts are collected by the Divine. Forgiveness frees up your own energy, which can be used for greater things than holding on to some past hurt. When you "give" a person who has caused you pain back to God, you liberate your own psyche and make your energy available for your own evolution.

A wounded heart closes up to protect itself. You'll notice people who fold their arms in front of their chests, as if to say, "I'm not open to you." Sadly, too many of us have become wound experts. We hug our experiences of abuse, addiction, betrayal, and childhood trauma close to our hearts as if our wounds were the primary facet of our identity. Many people live in this closed state their entire lives. When the heart clogs up for long periods of time, something big often has to happen to blow it all out at once and open us once more to life. Serious illness, especially heart attacks, may be one form this blowout takes. Unfortunately, it's often in crisis that families are the closest, and much forgiveness and real transformation happens when the wounds of the heart are openly shared.

If this Seed Thought is speaking to you, you may be living in denial about the effects of some unhealed heart wound. Denial, as we have seen, often leads to projection. You may be blaming someone in your current life for some past hurt that you've been unable to acknowledge. A clue that this is what's happening is that you find yourself engaging in incessant arguments with someone over the same old theme or feel yourself to be caught in a repeating pattern of negative reactivity that bounces back and forth between you and gets you nowhere.

Getting clear about what's past and what's present is the first step in healing this problem. Take a moment and ask yourself what emotional hurts you may still need to heal. Whom do you still need to forgive? Can you love yourself enough to work through any past grief and move on into the future? Once you know what you're facing, you must take action to clear the fog off your mirror. Sacred heartwork may require that you call a friend or family member and set up a time to engage in a heart-to-heart dialogue about any unfinished business between you.

An unhealed wound from the past may also cause you to "protect" yourself so as not to be wounded again in the future. Ask yourself whether and in what ways this may be true for you. Are you holding yourself back from some new opportunity that is inviting you to step beyond your familiar ways because you are scared you won't measure up? Did some authority figure in the past make you feel as if you'd failed? Or are you scared you may have to give up something you feel you cannot do without?

Remind yourself that it's natural to feel anxiety when you start to expand beyond your usual parameters. Opening your heart to compassion for yourself can help you tolerate the tension of not knowing how things will turn out. Think of how courageous you've already been to have made it to this stage of awakening. Know that it's time now to trust the process of evolution to carry you forward to your next right place. I've learned that when we do our part and open, God will do the rest.

As you practice the work of coming from the heart, one day you will see that you've developed the ability to live from the heart in all situations. You will have stepped out from behind the veil of superficiality, no longer afraid to be truly yourself. You know people who behave this way. So do I. They are a joy to be around and model for us the beauty of authentic living.

The following process can help you clear the wounds of the heart and move you toward this more open and courageous approach to life.

Exercise
Surrender into Love

Read this exercise all the way through before you practice it. If music helps to activate your emotions, put on some evocative music without words, close your eyes, and allow yourself to go quietly into your feelings.

Feel the sadness or hurt, the fear, the sense of betrayal. Whatever is in your heart, let it come. . . . Now give yourself permission to grieve your feelings in any way that feels appropriate. Cry, beat a pillow, shout at the heavens, make low groaning sounds coming from deep in your chest. . . . Since anger may also be involved in your feelings, express your anger in some nonhurtful way. Yell, stamp your feet, or dance out your fury. . . . Allow all of the energy of any feelings you may have repressed to move through you and out now. . . .

As you bring the emotion through, imagine that a soft white light is entering your heart from the sky of mind. See that your mind is connecting with your heart, inviting it to relax and open. Concentrate on this light flooding into your heart until you experience a gradual lightening of your feelings. Using your creative imagination, continue to let your heart fill with this light until you are completely relaxed and calm. Now stay with this feeling of lightness and release until your chest cavity empties and you feel transparent. . . . Take as long as you need for this process to subside. . . .

Let the music play for a while now, and when all your emotions are clear, notice how much lighter you feel. As you go back to your usual routines, you may notice a dramatic improvement in your emotional responsiveness and your clarity of mind.

Anytime you feel that your heart is clogging up with unexpressed feeling, know that you can repeat this exercise in emotional release.

These last three Seed Thoughts helped you to integrate your mental body so that your will to know is strong enough to lead you upward into the spiritual realms. Now you are becoming capable of right thought. The higher cognitions of the creative imagination, inspiration, and intuition can open to you, because the elements of earth, water, and air have been owned and integrated. From this place, you will step more confidently into the life of the Spirit knowing that your ego and personality are ready to harmonize with your soul.

Seed Thought Ten
**Your symptoms of distress are not pathological;
they are the natural pangs of birthing
a new consciousness.**

Birthing new aspects of yourself can be as agonizing as physically giving birth. The symptoms of distress you may experience during this process are not pathological. Rather, they are the natural labor pains that accompany the birth of a more profound awareness. Like the caterpillar transforming within its chrysalis so that it can be remade into a butterfly, or a snake shedding the skin it has outgrown, transformations of consciousness are seldom easy or pretty. Any birth entails a certain amount of suffering as the membranes of the familiar are stretched into new forms.

You can never prepare sufficiently for the rapid changes personal transformation may bring. Sequences of death/rebirth actually define the word *transformation*. As you watch your familiar life spin out of control, you may feel shocked or frightened, even when the changes under way are ones you wished for or helped to initiate. Once the forces of transformation are set in motion, they seem to take over, and you can only watch as everything you knew comes apart so that new life can come into being. Psyche went through this process in her final task, as she entered the underworld to die to her old identity and to be reborn as the goddess she was destined to be.

Actually, you are always dying to your old self and being reborn into new states of awareness. Seen in the light of the spiritual psychology we have been developing, each time you enter the personal underworld of a life crisis, some unneeded part of you dies so that you can be reborn to a larger life. But if you can view the necessary discomforts of the process as labor pains rather than as pathological symptoms, you can keep yourself moving forward in a positive direction.

Conventional psychology has not trained you to understand that cycles of death and rebirth are basic to your nature. Since this misunderstanding has colored your perceptions, you may be squeamish about calling the natural ending of some aspect of your life a "death." It's hard to be reminded that every living thing will someday die—even you! So it's somehow easier to think, when a marriage or relationship ends, or you lose your job or suffer some other financial reversal, that you've failed in some way. You blame yourself, or are blamed by others, for making a mistake, for being incompetent, for not putting in enough effort. As a result, when parts of your life die, your self-esteem drops, and you're convinced that you've done something wrong. What's worse, some conventional doctors and therapists validate this disempowering self-judgment by pathologizing your grief or depression and prescribing drugs or other palliatives for your so-called symptoms.

You may also hesitate to call the new beginnings you experience "rebirths," yet that's what they are. Most of you reading this book have already been "reborn" several times—during *this lifetime*. Take a moment to remember some of those occasions—a recovery from an addiction or a life-threatening illness, a new relationship rising from the ashes of a love life that seemed over after a bitter divorce, a bold new job in a new city—and you'll see what I mean.

As you go through these perfectly natural cycles of death and rebirth, there are a few things that are important to keep in mind. First, the process of giving birth to a new self must be given its appropriate time. Psychospiritual births are not tied to a nine-month cycle. They can happen instantaneously, or they can take several years. Soul transformations take place in *kairos* time, "soul time" that unfolds at its own speed. They cannot be hurried or rushed.

Second, you may notice physical changes that mirror this

internal process. I've noticed that when I'm in a death cycle, my face takes on a yellowish pallor and all my days are bad hair days. When the cycle starts shifting into the rebirth phase, my color returns, my eyes brighten, and my body experiences newfound energy. Physically it's easy to track these times, for they are usually quite obvious.

Finally, it's important to remember that rebirth always follows the death part of the cycle. No matter how black the world looks when you've suffered some loss, there is one thing you can count on absolutely. Even the most devastating emotional pain eventually ends. You *will* feel different to-morrow—maybe worse, maybe better, but certainly different from what you feel today. Even a moment's thought about the cycles of nature will also convince you that life always wins out over death. Broken hearts mend; shattered lives reconstellate into new forms; and from under the smoldering cinders of a forest fire, new green shoots are already starting to reach toward the sky.

Though ordinary life will provide you with plenty of op-portunities to practice rebirth, Eupsyschia's workshop inten-sives provide a context for this sacred process and help participants make the birth sequence overt. Using a com-bination of music therapy and breathwork, participants ac-cess perinatal consciousness and relive the actual felt experience of their biological birth. It's amazing and won-derful to watch people struggling to get born. They choke; they gurgle; they cry out in infant rage. Once the process of birth takes hold, they need encouragement to come on through, and usually someone to hold on to, to comfort them and help them push. And what relief when these energies subside and the person comes to consciousness in a brand-new world! The moment of rebirth is always a celebration and a blessing!

The rebirthing process can also be carried out by ritual and symbol. One of the most touching examples of this courageous undertaking happened at a Eupsychia healing intensive with a woman I'll call Emily. A victim of severe childhood abuse, Emily was living out of her body so much that she couldn't stay grounded enough to work. Many times, with dozens of dolls and other objects as concrete reminders, she had gone back in time to relive her traumatic experiences with several of us supporting her.

As her memory started to return, our sessions with her became more intense, and Emily's mood started to shift. During one two-week intensive, she seemed to grow lighter every day. Clearly the rebirth part of the cycle was beginning. Then one evening we walked into the sacred space where we do our healing work and saw that Emily had brought to the altar the dolls and stuffed animals she'd used as symbols of her ordeal. She had stacked them into a pyramid as high as the burning candle in the center of the altar table. There she knelt, offering these tokens in reverent praise, as my staff and I stood tearfully by in deep respect. After that evening, we witnessed concrete changes in her demeanor and in her ability to stay grounded. Today, though she still has times of fragility, she lives comfortably in the ordinary world.

The closer you get to "home," the more treacherous the path and the more dangerous and difficult the work you must do. Since you are coming closer to the core, your deepest issues will arise to be healed. Yet, paradoxically, the journey gets easier near the end. For one thing, you've learned so much by now, through all the work you've done. What's more, you've probably found yourself to be in the congenial company of fellow seekers. These people feel so familiar, you feel you've known them always. So rest assured, if you are new to the sacred path, that you are not alone. Soon you will find your spiritual family, whose loving support will help your faith and courage to bloom.

Everyone is evolving. But those who have made the process of their own evolution conscious and are pursuing transformational work tend to "go first." The majority change more slowly, in tune with society's more gradual pace of growth. They mature through life's natural ups and downs. You'll know if you are among those who have chosen to participate in the divine experiment of a rapid transformation. Perhaps you've embarked on a course of spiritual study, or have signed up for a year of intensive transformational or healing work.

If you are traveling this accelerated path, your soul will never allow you to rest in a state of stasis. Knowing that transformation requires stirring the pot, your soul will jolt you out of any complacency through some conflict or crisis. Watch and you will see! As a volunteer for this accelerated path, you're destined to grow by leaps and bounds, discontinuous shifts in consciousness that can be quite disconcerting. Sequences of death and rebirth are much more dramatic than a continuum of incremental growth. You can protest noisily when the next death and rebirth cycle is upon you, or you can relax and go with the flow, trusting in the process itself as the sacred service you've signed on for.

Remember, it's your own soul that has volunteered for this path. You heard the call to grow in consciousness, and you responded. Dying to the old is certainly painful, but its other side is evolution itself—the birth pangs all initiates experience as they prepare themselves to be part of a new humanity.

LIFE LESSON

Befriending Death

If this Seed Thought seems particularly significant, you may have hit one of these times when Death is knocking at your psychic door, saying, "It is finished. Come with me." Though you may wish to grab on to something familiar and hang on with all your might, you'll feel the ground slipping out from under your feet, as some new way calls you to move on. Death can be a friend, though it's sometimes quite difficult to appreciate this fact.

If you're like me, relationships are the hardest thing to see die. If a significant relationship is dying for you right now, be honest with the person with whom the thread of connection is breaking. Tell this person about the shift you need to make in ways that do not sound as though you are blaming. Own your part in every situation that needs completing and have the courage to accept your responsibility for what is happening. Your honesty will free the other person to be absolutely straightforward with you.

Sometimes a miracle will happen when you hit a rock-bottom place with someone significant in your life. An entire relationship can turn a corner, even continue rather than end, because the internal dynamic has shifted so much that, though the same two people are involved, the relationship between them has been reborn in a new form. I've seen this happen many times. So have the courage to let die what needs to, in complete honesty, and then allow whatever needs to happen to take form.

Perhaps the death you're facing is a career shift or a way of life that is passing away. You may be facing retirement, or your children may be leaving home, or you may be selling the home you've lived in most of your life. This kind of change can be very scary, until you learn to let go and allow the process to continue. If your new way of living is still unformed, you may need to spend some time just gestating, to give the new life a chance to take shape. Don't try to force things or push too much. And remember, the old way must die to make room for the new. Never hold on to the corpse of your old way of living past its time. Give things away. Plan a trip. Make an empty room into a studio or a meditation room. Remember that in her final task Psyche was warned not to try to rescue the dead man who would stretch out his rotting hand to her as she crossed the river Styx.

Finally, listen carefully to what is trying to happen. One of the gravest errors people can make is thinking that an outer change in relationship, career, or geography is what's needed, when all along what was really called for was an inner shift in attitude or priorities. The trick to telling the difference is to start with small, inner changes, waiting to see what difference each makes. If you begin with yourself and work the process from the inside out, you can often hold off from making radical shifts that change your life irrevocably. When any outer condition needs to change, you'll know it with no lingering doubts. When you give the process time to unfold, new opportunities may also appear that make it a little easier to move on.

The key to this lesson is to see any painful or unsuccessful situation as part of a cycle of death and rebirth rather than as a failure. Let go what needs to die. Focus on what's coming, rather than on what's leaving. This kind of thinking will turn you away from your past and toward your emerging future. Don't panic and do something drastic! Just let the process have its way with you—consciously, of course. And when the going gets rough, remember, life always wins! The following exercise can help you through your times of transition:

Exercise
Hanging in the Dangle

When your old life dies and the new has not yet arrived, you learn the art of "hanging in the dangle." This phrase was coined in an interchange with a group of my students in Georgia about fifteen years ago. Several in the group had announced that they were living in their cars. These folks had been striving so hard to create new lives that they had made choices that were not logical, giving up their only means of making a living before the new way had announced itself! The frustration in the group was high, when someone who had gone on and on in her complaining finally cried out, "I feel like I'm just dangling in the middle of nowhere!"

"Well, I guess you'll just have to hang in the dangle," I replied with some irritation, which immediately became funny and gave us all a good laugh.

If this feeling of sitting on a fence post between two lives is happening to you right now, get busy learning the skill of how to hang out in that state of no-place-to-be. Believe it or not, you can learn to relax into this particular stage on the journey, especially if you have a few loving friends who will support your process and help you feel less anxious or ungrounded.

It helps to envision yourself as the trapeze artist who has let go of one bar and is reaching for the other that has not quite arrived. Tell yourself that there's a safety net underneath you—that if you fall, you'll be caught. This safety net is the context of transformation itself. As you've learned, metamorphosis is movement. You know that no matter what happens, things will change. Even fear or despair will eventually drop away. Later, you'll look back and see that this moment of hanging in the dangle was terrifying but also purposeful and exhilarating. In the open moment, anything can happen, and something certainly will!

Here is a process that can help support you through this awkward stage:

- Focus with all your might on your spiritual intention.
- Imagine that your personal vibration matches the energy of the Higher Power.
- Consciously surrender to this higher vibration knowing that it can move through you.
- Now just let go.
- Stay in the presence of your Higher Power or inner guide no matter what is happening. Trust that the process of new birth is under way.
- Wait patiently and recognize your new life as it begins to show.
- Be willing to take the first step into your new life, no matter how vulnerable or ill prepared you feel. Just do it! And you'll be on your way.

Seed Thought Eleven
Sacrifice is not a giving up but a taking on.

When we first commit to the spiritual path, we have no idea what's in store for us. We expect that life will get better simply because we've decided to become spiritual. As Psyche showed us, however, it's not quite like that. We say to ourselves, at first, in innocence, "Okay. I am willing." But once we turn our life over to a Higher Power, events unfold in ways we cannot always control. Often I hear from participants at our Eupsychia trainings: "I saw the brochure, and I just knew I had to be here." Or "I threw away the brochure, but it just kept reappearing!" Later they tell me that coming to one of these events began a process that led to finding their life's work, connecting with a new soul friend, or discovering some missing piece that clarified their life story.

This shift from ego-dominated to soul-based living is not an intellectual decision. It is a process brought about through the great law of sacrifice, beyond your ego's control. The law of sacrifice is the divine principle that powers the transformational process. It's the call you receive over and over to surrender the lesser to the greater, to release energy that has been imprisoned in your emotional body and use it for a higher good.

The impulse to start living spiritually signals that the seeds of Divine Life planted in your consciousness have now started to sprout. Your soul picks up this impulse and wills you to sacrifice anything that's in the way of the next step of your journey. For instance, it may ask you to separate from an obsessive attachment that may have claimed your energy in the past, such as an addiction, a codependent or dysfunctional relationship, or a recurring pattern of negative thinking. To peel away these limiting patterns, you must surrender your personal will to a Higher Power. Such surrender is not a giving up of power or control. Rather, it is a taking on of the soul strength that puts your Higher Self in charge and moves you to some greater responsibility or intent.

Oftentimes we think that we've surrendered something just because we've thought about doing it, or proclaimed it in words. I first observed this phenomenon when I was an adolescent attending meetings of Al-Anon, the self-help organization for family members of alcoholics. As we'd sit in our circle and share our stories, I would hear the wife of an alcoholic say, "I've surrendered my need to control my husband's drinking. I am letting go and letting God." But then, many times I'd notice that despite the woman's avowal of surrender, she would start to talk about her husband in a way that revealed that she was still preoccupied with controlling his behavior. I remember thinking, "That doesn't sound like surrender to me," and I would puzzle over what surrender really meant.

Later I realized that those declarations of surrender were well-intentioned aspects of the Alcoholics Anonymous strategy, seed thoughts being planted in the minds of people who were not yet ready to make genuine changes. Only when a person makes a felt shift in consciousness can the conversion experience of real surrender occur. Then old habits of thinking are truly sacrificed, and life is transformed.

You'll know when you're in a cycle of surrender. You may start to feel as if you are butting your head against some situation in your life so violently that it's making you physically sick. Nothing makes sense, and the harder you try to sort things out, the worse it gets. Other times, surrender may be signaled by an unexpected act of disobedience in which you suddenly find yourself acting in a way you never planned. Psyche's opening the jar of Persephone's beauty ointment was this kind of surrender. So was the time I announced to my husband that I was leaving him, just after I'd made a firm decision to stay. After a real surrender, you may experience a feeling of lightness, as if some burden has truly been lifted.

Though we often point to one event or one moment and

identify it as our surrender, letting go is generally a process that unfolds in stages.

The first stage is the recognition that something—a habit or addiction, an attitude or belief, an attachment to some person in your life—is holding you back from fulfilling your higher calling.

Second, you'll start talking to your friends or loved ones about what you need to change or let go. Often they will validate your decision.

The third stage is generally a time of vacillation. You'll quit smoking and then start again, for instance, with much contention between warring parts of yourself. Or you'll decide to stop obsessing about an old relationship but find that all you do is talk about it. During this stage you often feel as if you're not getting anywhere and may seek help of some kind. What you may not realize consciously is that you are building up steam.

In the fourth stage, you will start to realize how crucial this sacrifice is, and you'll fully commit to carrying it out. Now the full surrender process will take hold and, if you do not block it, will move you through. You may grieve or feel scared or lost, while you mentally build your determination to persevere. Journaling these feelings and insights can help you release whatever you're holding on to more quickly and easily.

When the fifth stage hits, you'll start to implement the change you are seeking, usually one small step at a time. Once the process gets this far, miracles or synchronicities often begin to happen. You'll receive a gift of money that helps you carry out your plan; a new person comes into your life; or an offer of an unanticipated new job comes through. Once we commit to a needed sacrifice, it's as though the gods hear our plea and help us set up a whole new way of being.

I experienced each of these stages in a surrender of my own several years ago, with life-changing results. I had inherited the business side of my national training program, which I did not know how to handle, and was on the brink of financial disaster. I had poured my heart into this work. I was so attached that I kept running up debt, justifying my poor decisions with magical thinking that continued the downward spiral, trying hard to ignore the seriousness of the situation. Finally, I could no longer live in delusion and realized that it was time to quit. I talked to several good friends and went through the anguish of accepting what it meant to let go.

In a spirit of calm surrender, I arranged a meeting between my lawyer, my CPA, and my business manager to discuss declaring bankruptcy. My son, a consultant for a large business firm in Houston, decided at the last minute to attend the meeting as well. Soberly, we convened in my lawyer's office and began to discuss the drastic effects this action would have. Then, to my surprise, my son took over the meeting, and said, "My mother is not going bankrupt. This company is her life's work, and it must continue." With that, he wrote the check that put us back on track. Such love, such joy spread through that room! It was as though a phoenix had miraculously arisen from the ashes.

From that point, and with my willingness to be a more responsible director, Eupsychia began a cycle of rebirth. It may die again tomorrow. Cycles come and go. But right now, we are very much alive. The divine law of sacrifice is relentless in its demand that our refinement perpetually continue. When you think about it, how else could evolution work?

Usually you need to let go of only one piece of your life at a time. But sometimes a whole way of being dies at once. If this ever happens to you, it's important that you get some support, as the symptoms can be quite severe. You may experience physical illnesses that medical science cannot diagnose, including rapid loss or gain of weight, eyesight problems, nervous disorders, or changes in appearance you can't explain. Emotional shifts may also occur, such as crying a lot, when you rarely cry, or being scattered and flighty, when you're known for being so together. Or a depression can set in, and you'll lose interest in your career, your friends, your usual social life, or your hobbies. These changes may cause an out-of-control feeling that can make you fear you're really losing it. You find yourself hanging in the dangle, with your old life completely shattered and nothing yet on your awareness screen that vaguely resembles a new one.

On a higher level, here's what's happening: Your soul is purifying you. It is busy clearing your lower three chakras where your needs for security, sensual or emotional gratification, and self-esteem reside. Everything familiar is being stripped away so that there's space in your life for something new to come in. Take heart! Gradually your creative imagination will ignite, and you'll feel inspired once more. And even though the pieces of your new life may not have fallen into place, intuitively you'll just know you are on the right track.

Psyche modeled this kind of complete ego death for us when she opened Persephone's jar. Now, why, we might well ask, would she sacrifice her final victory and even her life, just so she could look beautiful for her lover? When we look at her actions on a deeper level, however, it becomes clear that Psyche's disobedience represents the final battle between her human vanity and her soul's sacred purpose. Sacrifice always involves such a confrontation. The ego holds on to some attachment, while the soul is pushing one toward some higher attainment. And if you'll notice, it took both her human vanity and her soul's spiritual intent to create the miracle that ensued.

Psyche's act of disobedience was, in fact, an act of heroism. Divine Beauty does not belong only to the gods. In opening Persephone's jar, Psyche was bringing Divine Beauty to the human realm. The domain where the new goddess Psyche would reign was neither the underworld nor the Olympian realm but the earth—the domain of *your* psyche and mine. In giving up her old self—and even her life—and taking on her higher calling, the mortal Psyche died and a divine/human goddess of love and beauty was born.

So pay attention to this mythic story, for a similar call to surrender may happen to you at some point along your sacred journey. Like Psyche, you came from the heaven world to bring your gift to this earth. Never forget this! We are all Psyche. Initiation into higher consciousness requires that we die to our lesser self so that our Higher Self can take charge and the Divine can begin to work through us.

Sacrificing the lesser for the greater is all that our Higher Self ever asks of us. When we are courageous enough to say "I am willing" and really mean it, we'll be spun into a whole new stage of our unfolding. With each sacrifice, we gain the strength to focus more and more on the soul's story and to experience the freedom of living life as a conscious divine/human being!

LIFE LESSON

Making the U-turn and Heading Home

If this Seed Thought is hitting home with you, the time may have come for you to let go of some outworn attachment. You may be feeling a strong pull to turn in a new direction, but you haven't yet started to move. When you enter the path of return to your Source, evolution itself is guiding you toward fulfilling your life's purpose. As you hang there on the threshold of this new life, you realize that you must let evolution "do you" rather than being attached to the idea that you are "doing it."

The intellect alone cannot decide what you need to do to support the next stage of your awakening. Your intellect is an organizing mind only. It has no way to figure out the future except by what has happened in the past. Therefore the ego is not creative. So when a time of surrender is upon you, you must relinquish your ego's ways of knowing, such as intellectual comparisons, judgment, and analysis, and cultivate a steady willingness to respond to your psyche's higher processes, creative imagination, inspiration, and divine intuition.

The key to approaching life in this higher way is to travel light. Usually what you're required to sacrifice is a stance or opinion of some kind. When your internal dialogue includes such phrases as "I never . . ." or "I always . . ." or "I have the right to . . ." it's a tip-off that some part of your personal history has hardened into a limiting attitude that has become part of you. Letting go of these attitudes is terribly difficult. "That's just how it is," we say, never having questioned our long-held opinion as being the only truth.

I had a client once whose mother abandoned the family when he was three. Every time he began a relationship with a woman, he behaved in insecure ways, questioning her excessively or accusing her of being unfaithful when there was no evidence that this was the case. This man's emotional body had to learn that all women were not his mother. Until he surrendered his anger and his fear of being abandoned again, he would never be able to sustain a healthy relationship.

Every relationship, if lived through consciously, will help us to surrender our attachment to romantic illusions that are really unmet needs masquerading as love. So often in my workshops I hear the stories of women who have fallen in love with a *puer aeternus*, an eternal youth. These men refuse to grow up and often seduce a mother figure into taking care of them. One story in particular illustrates the healing that comes of surrendering such unhealthy attractions.

Meredith was a talented photographer in her mid-forties. She had been supporting a man we'll call Jon whose own photographic work never seemed to bring in money. He spent most of his time photographing penniless wanna-be models, eating in expensive restaurants, and shopping for luxuries. However, Jon was so charming that Meredith could not seem to break the pattern of supporting him. Though her head knew it was time to let go and move on, her heart would not cooperate. She held on to the belief that he loved her and that though he found it difficult to show it, inside he was deeply grateful for her devotion and support.

Then one day Jon announced that he had fallen in love with a woman half his age and was moving in with her. Meredith was grief stricken. Even though Jon had abandoned her, much as the young Eros—the archetypal *puer*—had abandoned Psyche, she could not let go of her attachment. After months of not being able to figure out what to do, Meredith's intuition led her to a Eupsychia healing intensive. At first, all she could do was surrender to her grief. Then, one by one, she gave up the illusions she had held about her relationship with Jon and began to accept responsibility for the part she had played in creating and continuing the unhealthy connection. Like Psyche, her own soul learning led Meredith to a deeper understanding of the true nature of love. Now alert to the dangers of men who are really perpetual little boys, Meredith vowed to love with her eyes open next time and to avoid emotional entanglements that limit her own full expression.

Perhaps some limiting belief is holding you back. For instance, you might be nursing a grudge against a co-worker who once betrayed you. This grudge is your ego's way of staying hooked and of forcing you to carry around unnecessary baggage. Your anger and resentment may be eating up so much of your precious psychic energy that you have lost the ability to think creatively. The higher qualities of acceptance and forgiveness may seem forever beyond your reach. Anything you're holding on to from the past—any psychological unfinished business—burdens the psyche and wastes the energy you should be using to advance along your path.

So ask yourself:

- What outmoded judgment or opinion am I still carrying?
- What does maintaining this stance do for me?
- What am I afraid might happen if I let go?
- Is there a pattern to the kind of mate or co-worker I seek?

The key to this lesson in love is losing your fear of surrendering to the unknown, so that the mystery of life can bless you. When you live in surrender, you open yourself to what the ancients knew as spiritual alchemy, which perpetually transforms the dross of your life into gold.

Exercise

Shifting from Horizontal to Vertical Dimension

Sacrificing some old attachment or identity can signal a time for turning inward and receiving messages from your soul. Your own consciousness completes the U-turn by shifting from the worldly horizontal plane that unfolds along a time line of past, present, and future, to the sacred inner vertical dimension that unfolds beyond time and space. When you shift to the vertical perspective, instead of looking outward, your focus is upward or inward.

Here are the steps you can follow if you're ready to make this shift:

- Find a quiet place where you won't be disturbed and become very still.
- Bring to mind an image of your Higher Power.
- Image yourself standing at the intersection of a cross, at the point where the horizontal and the vertical lines meet.
- Look up and offer whatever you are releasing with open hands. Really feel what you are giving up leave your hands.
- If tears or feelings come, allow them to flow unimpeded until they naturally subside.
- Thank your Higher Power for this opportunity to sacrifice this part of yourself that you no longer need.
- Sit in the void this loss creates and feel the emptiness. Be willing to stay with this feeling for a while.
- Take a moment to envision yourself living without this attachment.

- When the time feels right, allow the emptiness to be filled with a sense of joy and relief. Breathe in this lighthearted feeling. Make it real.
- Now in your mind, see yourself moving on—lighter, unburdened, and free.

Seed Thought Twelve
**As you cultivate your own nature,
all around you begins to grow.**

You have come so far on your sacred journey! By now, you have entered into an intimate relationship with your soul. Yet there is one more step to take. It is time to bring to consciousness your ultimate means of serving humanity. The secret of true service is simple: develop your own qualities to their highest level—achieve your own soul's fulfillment—and the light of Spirit will express itself through everything you do so that all of humanity is served.

When you first hear this Seed Thought, you might think, "That's ridiculous! How can fulfilling my own purpose help others?" But reflect a bit more deeply, and you'll see that when your life is guided from within by its highest principles, the extraordinary shines through the ordinary everywhere you look. This insight brings a sense of sacred meaning and purpose to all of your activities and helps to spiritualize the material world.

This same Seed Thought has inspired the life of every

sacred world server, who can be our models for doing our part. When the Buddha sat down under the bodhi tree vowing not to move until he achieved enlightenment, what was he doing but fulfilling his own purpose? Because he did so, he was able to teach others to follow his example and escape the world's suffering. Jesus, too, in fulfilling his own spiritual destiny, provided the supreme example of selfless world service. Because he was willing to know himself, he was able to guide all of us, as the Gospel According to Thomas reminds us: "Whosoever knows the All but fails to know himself lacks everything."

Those of you who know yourself to be initiates recognize that wherever you are on your journey to awakening, you carry within you the fetus of your own fully matured Higher Self. The seeds of wisdom, beauty, and love you have planted as you walk the path of direct experience have been gestating underground, in the dark night world of your consciousness. Watered by experience, nurtured by heartfelt self-awareness, these seeds of your own future flowering are now ready to burst into bloom. As you have worked through the lessons of *Psyche's Seeds*, your chakras have become more aligned and balanced. Now you can use their energy to birth whatever you wish—from a new self to a new world. You are clearing the fog from your inner mirror and bringing your energies into balance so that the process of manifestation can begin.

Everything you wish to create for yourself and for the world comes into being through a series of seven steps, beginning at the highest chakra and proceeding downward:

how to use psyche's seeds

- First, at the crown chakra, you conceive the idea.
- Second, at the third eye, you envision whether the idea will serve the highest good for you and for all humanity.
- Third, you use your creative imagination to transform the new idea into a formulated thought, giving it language at the throat chakra.
- Fourth, you surround your gestating new creation with the love and protection of your heart, as you would a precious child, desiring with all of your heart energy that it grow to healthy fruition.
- Fifth, at the solar plexus, you begin to devise concrete ways for this creation to materialize.
- Sixth, at the power center below your navel, you attract the helpers or tools that you need for the support and growth of the new creation.
- And finally, at the root chakra, you birth your new creation into the world.

Initiates do this process without even having to think about it. As an initiate-in-training, you can practice these steps until they become second nature.

Because you were raised in a materially oriented world, it may be hard for you to comprehend that the act of sacred self-creation is the key to everything you accomplish in life. You have been programmed to believe that the things that affect you are outer conditions. But every esoteric path teaches that the outer world is a world of appearances—the out-picturing of what we each have already planted in our minds and hearts. It is up to you to know whether this out-picturing mirrors your highest hopes and dreams or reflects those things you've obsessed or worried about! Clear minds and pure hearts make for heavenly creations.

You may also have been laboring under the mistaken notion that true service requires that you always put yourself last. That might sound very holy and unselfish, as no one wants to be self-centered or egoistic. But to live in self-forgetting before you've become a self is a violation of your psyche's ways. Until you have a strong sense of self, you have no self to give another person! To develop a true sense of self, you have to be self-preoccupied, at least for a while. You will always treat others as you treat yourself. If you neglect your own need for fulfillment, you'll neglect and mistreat others. The stages of growth move from selfish to selfhood to selfless. There is no shortcut through this process, though seekers on the accelerated path move through the stages at a quicker pace and often with more tension.

When you come to see this truth—and you will, if you do not already—the deep meaning of your incarnational journey will become clear. I remember once being in this state of realization. It seemed to me as if all the green trees, bushes, and flowers around my deck were reaching up toward the sky, waving their shiny leaves and blossoms, as though they were worshipping with deep reverence their right to be on earth! I felt I was part of this deep chorus of praise, my human-Divine Self dancing its incarnated joy. All was one. For that blessed moment, I felt I was in heaven here on earth.

The path of self-knowledge can never be learned from a

book or from listening to a lecture, no matter how wise the words you hear may be. It is by your own doing, as you've seen in these pages, that you learn, as Psyche did, to adapt to, integrate, and transcend your evolving identities as you take them on, and then, like skins that have become too tight, shed them so that you can expand. There will always be some aspect of your lower nature that you must leave behind, some part of you that is now too constricting to contain your burgeoning self. The Higher Self must use the lower self as raw material. Otherwise there's nothing for it to work with, no dross to turn into gold, no grist for the mill to transform. And so goes the process of awakening to who you truly are.

Sadly, many people get so captivated by their involvement in the mundane activities of the material world that they forget completely to focus on the real reason they're here. Once a young Vanderbilt graduate said to my son, "I know why I go to work every day. But what I don't know is why am I on this mud ball called earth?" It is usually as life nears its end that we hear people cry in bitter despair, "What have I really accomplished? Where did the time go? Is this all there is?"

But this will never be your cry if you awaken to the understanding that you have your own part to play as a facet of the glorious, unified Human Soul. You will understand that whatever experiences you pass through on your personal journey advance the cause of fulfilling the greater human purpose. This realization brings a strong sense of self-empowerment and just enough humility to keep the ego in check. You can safely say to yourself, "Nothing I do is ever just personal."

To learn to live as this paradoxical one who is both part and whole is your highest realization as a spiritual being in human form. I hope this book has brought this truth home to you. As you learn to honor both your inner and outer life as sacred and to travel consciously on your life journey, you become more willing to undertake both the joys and the travails that life brings. In this acceptance of what is, we reach fulfillment.

When she had completed her tasks, Psyche gave birth to the child she had been carrying, to whom she gave the name Joy. Her birth signaled the fulfillment of the mysterious mission Psyche had known intuitively was hers. You, too, can manifest a life of personal joy and fulfillment. Psyche has demonstrated for you the secret that completes any human journey toward individuation: when you are willing to focus intently on cultivating your own nature, everything else falls magically into place. Even when you don't realize this is what is happening, if you remain true to your course, in the end you come full circle, into your unique expression as a demonstrator of the Divine.

LIFE LESSON

Accepting the Mantle of Self-Empowerment

Through this Seed Thought you are called to stand tall in self-remembrance. You can live from your bigger story now, knowing you are participating in a divine world drama in which you play an essential role. You hold a piece of the jigsaw puzzle of human fulfillment. Without you, there's a hole in the picture that cannot be filled. When you accept the mantle of Divine Self–empowerment, your human biography will merge into the larger story of humanity's blossoming, and you will become more than you ever thought you could be.

A woman client I worked with a few years ago demonstrated beautifully how the principle of Divine Self-empowerment works. For weeks, she had been dreaming about being a person of great wisdom and beauty, fully dedicated to serving others. Her dreams rolled out before her imagination like Technicolor movie clips. She saw herself working in Africa with AIDS victims, feeding refugee children in Kosovo, and running a shelter for battered women in a large southern city. Her eyes shone as she described these visions. After listening to several of these dreams, I suggested that she try to act as if she really were this dedicated world server as she carried out the responsibilities of her ordinary life. One day she came to a session utterly radiant. She'd looked in the mirror that morning and saw herself as the Wise Woman she had been dreaming she could be. In accepting the mantle of self-empowerment, this woman had incarnated her most fully developed and fulfilled self.

Now all this may sound fanciful or just plain weird. Yet you are endowed with a spiritual body that is not subject to the laws of time and space. You live every day at the intersection between your ordinary human affairs unfolding horizontally in time and space, and simultaneoulsy the ever-present now of the Divine. Your Higher Self enters your life through the timeless vertical dimension. Each day, you move up and down along this vertical axis—sometimes dipping down to pull something up from your subconscious mind so that it can be acknowledged and healed; sometimes soaring into the unclouded sky of spiritual vision and ecstasy. Going down to pick up some lost part of yourself is as important and as sacred as flying to the heights. Anything you access on the vertical dimension furthers your integration.

The key to this lesson is letting go of any preconceived notions about who you are and what you can be. When you travel inward along the vertical dimension, you harvest the wisdom of experience gathered during every day of earthly life. In the light of the timeless now, you see that you have the power to heal the wounds of the past by redefining whatever has happened to you as a necessary step in your evolution. You can decide that each painful experience was designed to make you more skillful, more compassionate, or more authentic. Reframing your past in this way honors all that you have been and clears the path for your rapid progress toward a glorious future for yourself and for all humankind.

Becoming a Demonstrator of the Divine

As small children, we still retained our cosmic connection with Spirit. But as we grow and enter fully into everyday tasks, our cosmic memory starts to fade. When ordinary reality seems to be all there is, and those Soul Events during which everything shines with Spirit seem few and far between, you may need something to help you remember your greater identity and your real story. Whenever you feel the need to remind yourself of who you are in your fullness, you can use this simple exercise to banish any doubt or sense of limitation. It will enhance this experience if you will put on some quiet wordless inspirational music as a background for this experience:

Close your eyes and imagine that you are sitting outside on a beautiful starry night. . . . Feel the night breeze on your cheek and relax into a state of peaceful contentment. . . . Take as long as you need to imagine yourself fully into this scene. . . .

Now focus on one particular star in the indigo blue sky and imagine that it is so bright you can reach out and touch it. . . . See this star becoming brighter and brighter and beginning to move toward you. . . . As it comes closer, enfolding you in its light-filled beams of love, see that the star is really your own Divine Self, the fully realized one that all of your hard work on the sacred journey has brought to fruition. . . .

Now this Star-Self is merging with you and infusing you

with light . . . and you see the world you inhabit through new eyes. . . .

Standing in the light of the Star-Self that you are, you can easily see your life's work or life's purpose. . . . You see your part in the Divine Plan unfolding before you . . . and understand the role you are to play in opening a petal of humanity's blossoming for this particular time in human history. You can even see humanity in full bloom. . . .

Now just let this imagery take you wherever it might for a little while . . . and allow yourself to accept the mantle of your true mission and purpose for incarnating here on Earth. . . . Take as long as you need to anchor this knowing in your mind and heart. . . .

When you feel yourself coming back to ordinary reality, take a few moments to note in your journal what you have seen. Draw a cross on an empty page. Along the vertical line, make notes or draw images of yourself in your full flowering. On the horizontal line, make notes or draw images of your life's work and where you are along the path of its unfolding.

Then, in your mind, stand at the nil point where these two lines meet. Banish all self-doubt from your consciousness! Doubt is the final barrier you must cross before you can come home to yourself. You no longer need to carry old mental attachments. No blocks or negative thinking can stand in the way of your fulfillment as a human soul. Never forget that whatever is happening to you, you are and always will be a demonstrator of the Divine! The flowering of humanity depends on you.

giving birth to joy

As you can now appreciate, Psyche and Eros personify two aspects of your soul. As the dynamic muses in your psyche, this divine pair fills in the gap between your humanity and the Divine who spins the universe into being.

Psyche brings you the ability to perceive the world's beauty so that you can fall in love with it. Beauty enables us to see life poetically and artistically. When we see through Beauty's eyes, the dualism that divides us from the world's creations dissolves in a rush of unconditional love. Beauty is God's handwriting; it is love made visible. As the divine/human goddess of love and beauty, Psyche gives you the courage and the persistence to follow your dreams and to defy any authority that tries to come between you and your soul's desires.

Eros inspires you to unfold your life's true expression. Anytime you begin to lose interest in your soul's pursuits, Eros turns you on and makes you feel brand-new. Focusing your attention on the world's beauty and falling in love with it awakens the Eros principle in you, just as Psyche inspired Eros to rise from his sickbed and fly to her aid. The divine marriage between these two parts of the soul brings together all contraries and makes you whole.

The child born of the union of Psyche and Eros is a new archetype. She is the key to the mystery of uniting the mortal and immortal worlds, and the masculine and feminine principles in you. Joy, the child's name in the Olympian realms, is the natural expression of the soul's delight, the fruit of the highest mystical union. Her name on earth is Pleasure, which reminds us of the ecstasy and passion the human physical senses give us.

We are all to be the children of Psyche and Eros. As we consciously advance in our soul's journey on the path of direct experience, we learn to honor the inner and the outer, the dark and the light, the human and divine aspects of our nature. We come to understand that the purpose of our human incarnation is to allow the soul to shine through our physical being, so that heavenly Joy and earthly Pleasure can be felt as one.

spiritual psychology
comes of age

Ordinary psychology has little guidance to offer as we undertake this task. Most modern psychologies see human beings as flimsy egos ruled by a vast and mysterious unconscious, or as biological machines that can be fixed by the addition of chemical additives so that they work correctly. Moreover, Western psychotherapy generally considers only the events from the present moment backward in time to our birth as legitimate material for exploration. Anything beyond these bounds, including a psychological investigation of our relationship with the Divine, is usually considered a way to avoid working on our real issues, or else should be work for a priest and not a therapist.

However, as more and more contemporary practitioners are realizing, a genuine psychology must honor all that we are—the personal as well as the transpersonal, or spiritual, dimension. Only a spiritual psychology that takes into consideration our hybrid nature as being both human and divine can help us evoke the positive and the possible within us. The spiritual psychology I have been developing throughout this book holds that we have both an ego that governs our outer life and a soul that regulates our inner reality. Together ego and soul make up the self in its full and glorious expression. A psychology that ignores the soul does human nature a grave disservice. Because the soul is a full partner in making us who we are, a mystical experience is as legitimate a way to create an impact on the psyche as a good therapy session. In spiritual psychology, all levels of consciousness are honored as valuable pathways to personal well-being.

Spiritual psychology validates our search for meaning and spiritual purpose. Because it recognizes how big we are—the Divine, after all, is regarded as an innate aspect of our being—our quest for wholeness can take place both within our personal consciousness as well as within the collective mind of all humanity. Processes such as guided imagery, sacred theater, mythic journeys, movement, integrative breathwork, art therapy, and music therapy draw from the vast treasury of the world's cultural heritage to guide us into discovery of all that we contain. These curative arts will become predominate during this next cycle of our unfolding. The approach I have followed in this book—using the myth of Psyche and Eros as a vivid way to behold issues of our own awakening psyches—comes out of this orientation.

In the deep inner work we do with hundreds of clients and students every year, we've seen again and again that the human psyche is layered in bands of consciousness. As we deepen, this layered psyche begins to open from the surface of ourselves all the way to our core. Going within, we pass through the layers of memory of our personal biography where any traumas we experienced during our childhood or earlier life may appear to be made conscious and released. Below this level, our physical birth can be integrated and healed. Moving deeper, beyond the boundaries of our present personality, we move into the realm of past life memories. From there, time and space expand further, and we discover ourselves expressed within mythic and archetypal stories, such as the love story of Psyche and Eros. Finally, at our depths, we experience cosmic consciousness in which we recognize ourselves to be universal, spiritual beings. At our surface, we experience ourselves as individuals; at our source, we are the universe. Each of these levels has much to teach the awakening psyche. Each can help us become conscious of the patterns we contain—those that hold us back and those that encourage our transcendence.

This book has invited you to access each of these layers, with the belief that as you observe and focus, name and own, imagine and create, you will begin to feel more complete. As you do, it becomes easier and easier to allow yourself to be just exactly where you are in your process of awakening, without any sense of regret for not being "finished" yet. After all, full acceptance of yourself, no matter what, is the only perfection it makes sense to seek!

I've seen that there is only one way to get off the merry-go-round of negativity, low self-esteem, psychosomatic illness, and relationship woes: you must find something lofty within yourself to believe in and to hold dear. Inner spiritual experience—the sacred journey of your soul—is both your truth and your healer. Your spirituality is a psychological fact! When you open yourself to psyche, your soul's twin, your emotions and mind are transformed. This way of being spiritual grounds the sacred in a dynamic felt experience. No matter what religion or spiritual path you follow, you have the right to access Spirit directly, and every time you go within, you do.

Once you place God inside you, instead of out there on some remote cloud, your very identity begins to expand into the archetypal and transpersonal realms where mystical experiences abound. Spiritual experience lives within the collective human unconscious as well as in your personal soul. When you connect with the Divine Spirit within you, you are linked to every other seeker of truth and to all the wisdom that has ever been, and these experiences and insights will augment your own. Seen from this perspective, whatever formal spiritual practice you choose to follow becomes a truly magical event, in which both outer and inner realities are expressed and honored. Having bridged the gap between your mortal and immortal selves, "God work" will come easy to you, and you'll make rapid progress toward achieving both your spiritual and material goals. These deeper strata of humanity's mind deserve to be legitimized by a respected school of psychology. Our psychologies are having to expand because human beings are!

Psyche's story took place within that stage of evolution in which the relationship between the Divine and humankind was up to the whimsy of the gods. And even now, the Psyche/ Eros sacred union has yet to be realized here on earth. The problem of integrating the masculine and feminine within our nature has never been resolved. Having returned to Mt. Olympus, the kingdom of the gods, these archetypal lovers live only in the collective unconscious mind. Now the responsibility to heal into wholeness belongs to the human kingdom. We must be accountable for doing our human homework so that the archetypal and human kingdom can unite here on earth. For each of us to do our part, we can begin invoking Eros and Psyche to unify our minds and hearts. We can start to practice bringing soulful Joy and sensual Pleasure together in all our relations, and celebrate the Divine wherever we find it in the everyday happenings of our life. As I say all this to you, I am reminded of Abraham Maslow, the father of self-actualization theory, and the plea he made to his final class of students: "If not you," he said, "then who?"

epilogue

becoming a seed bearer

As I went by a pitch-pine wood the other day, I saw a few little ones springing up in a pasture from seeds which had been blown from the wood. . . . In a few years, if not disturbed, these seedlings will alter the face of Nature here.

—Henry David Thoreau, *Faith in a Seed*

A few years ago I had a vision that felt prophetic. I'd like to close by sharing it with you, for I believe that there is no spiritual vision that is "just personal." Spiritual psychology teaches us that whenever we enter a visionary state, we draw from our one Soul. Thus this vision belongs to all of us and points toward our collective future.

I saw myself rising out of the moist ground like a flower. I actually felt covered with mud, coming out of what I thought at first was a foxhole. For a moment I feared there had been a war, and the world had blown up. Then I realized that I was a tiny embryo, then a newborn, then a small child, gradually growing older as I crawled up a gentle, grassy hill. By the time I reached the top, I was a young girl, much like Psyche, standing on what seemed to be a new earth.

The terrain of this earth was different somehow, and as I looked around, I saw why. There was nothing artificial here. All telephone wires, asphalt parking lots, and buildings—everything mechanical or manufactured by human hands had vanished. The earth was a garden, vibrant with blooming flowers, green bushes, and trees. The sky above was a deep blue, until it reached the horizon. There it turned a gorgeous indigo-rose, a color I've never seen here on earth. A moment of panic ran through my body when I noticed that no one was around. "Am I the only survivor? Has the world I've known been destroyed?"

Then I heard the shouting of a crowd of happy people, and I realized we were all there, gazing at this magnificent green world, jubilant in our celebration that we'd completed the job we'd come here to do. Then the most compelling music burst forth from Mother Earth herself, so sensual, powerful, rhythmic, and melodic it shook my soul. It sounded like a medley of primal drumming and cosmic rock and roll—so sensual, and with a melody line that seemed to encompass every human experience. I knew this music expressed the very essence of earth life, a perfect sound track for what we'd come here to be.

Then I looked up in the sky and saw several celestial beings coming toward us from a higher world. To me they appeared as the Christ or some other Great Messenger in the center, with a legion of angels or high beings surrounding him. I knew that they were all archetypes, ethereal beings of a higher order than we'd known in human form.

As the beings drew closer I could hear a celestial music surrounding them, majestic and harmonious, beautiful high minor chords that melted into the earth's sensuous melody and beat. As these two musical compositions merged, the vibration was profoundly moving. I could feel it all the way through my skin.

As if carried by the music of blending heaven and earth, the celestial beings began to melt into all of us as we stood there to greet them. They were made of energy and light, so they melted into our human bodies with ease. I felt this happening in my own body, and a quickening in my mind and heart. I'm certain the others felt this as well. Then, as this new creation we had so magically become, we all turned toward the radiant western sky and together walked toward the new horizon. I knew at that moment that as we advance into full participation in the spiritual dimension, nothing that is humanly good will ever be lost.

Today we are standing at the entrance of a brand-new era in our human history, and we are its seed bearers. Psyche's triumph and her love for Eros is an inner event that has profoundly affected humankind. The mystery of high love has captivated our psychic development for at least two thousand years, evidenced in every culture's art and religion. And we know there is no mistaking this potent insight. For don't we all live this mystery in our own minds and hearts? In times to come, body and Spirit will merge, and we will bring heaven to earth. As Psyche's quest for love affirms, humans will someday be as gods, and gods will live in mortal skin.

And so ends this tale of the marriage of a human with a god. Or is this perhaps a new beginning upon a higher plane?

index

"acting in" versus acting out, 192

addictions, 42, 53, 152, 160, 188, 190. *See also* compulsions

Al-Anon, 236–37

altruistic wish to help, as trap, 110–11

"always," 158

anima and *animus*, 169

ants, 57

Aphrodite, 29, 30, 47, 48, 51, 55, 59, 68, 85, 87, 89, 106, 107, 121

archetypes, 10, 12, 20, 92, 140. *See also* symbols

attachment. *See* "I am" letting go of, 117, 161–65, 246

awareness, 42–43

Beauty, 140, 241, 257

beauty, 55, 118, 129

Bhagavad Gita, 148

birth, 252. *See also* death(s); self, that one was born to be

birthing a new consciousness, 225–30

breathwork, 191

Buddha, the, 41, 248

chakra(s), 60–61, 78, 248–49
  second, 78–79
  third, 97–98
  three upper, spiritual, 98, 118–19, 128–29, 216

codependence, 111

compassion, 179, 217

compulsions, 188–90. *See also* addictions

consciousness, 210
  birthing a new, 225–30
  coming to, 152
  journey to, 137
  observer, 95, 96

creativity, 79, 96

cults, 54

daily practice, notes about, 66–67, 82–85

Death, 107

death-in-life state, 116
death(s), 114
    befriending, 231–33
    birth(s), rebirthing, and, 18–21,
        23, 226–27, 230–31, 233
    as illusion, 20
    painful endings as, 42
Demeter, 48
denial, 80, 81, 107, 108, 222
desire, capacity for, 186
desire nature, 186–93
destiny, 113, 126
diary, spiritual. *See* journal
discernment and discriminating
        vision, 56–57, 94–95. *See also*
        order, creating
disidentification, 165–66, 246
disobedience, 241
distress. *See* suffering
    and birthing a new consciousness,
        225–31
Divine, 8, 219–20
    demonstrating the, 255–56
    open heart and the, 105, 216–20
Divine Child, 20
Divine Self, 148, 149, 156, 158, 165,
        182
Divine Self-empowerment, 253
dogs, in myth, 111, 112
"dragon" energy and "hungry
        dragon," 75–76
dualism and duality, 140, 199. *See*
        also opposites
    resolving the mystery of, 142–44

ego, 90, 91, 138, 139, 143, 154
    death/relinquishment of, 241,
        243
    needy, 6, 187, 188
ego container, 88–93

ego integration, 98
emotional/creative force, making
        right use of, 80–82
emotional expression and release
        work, 92, 191, 224
empowered self, 183–86. *See also* self-
        empowerment
enantiodromia, 73–74
Eros, invoking, 195–97
Eros principle, 129
Eupsychia, 141, 171, 180, 191, 228,
        229, 235, 240, 244
eupsychia, 3

fairy tales, 105–6, 116
false self, 28
false spirituality, 54
fate. *See* destiny
female-dependent men, 47
Feminine, Divine, 29, 115
feminine principle, 120, 200
femininity, 46. *See also* masculinity
        and femininity
    dark, 106, 108
    mature, 106, 107
forgiveness, 179, 185, 221, 245
freedom of thought, reclaiming,
        184–86

Ganymede, 89
gender divide. *See* masculinity and
        femininity
    communicating across, 202
Gnostic Christian Gospels, 139
God, 138. *See also* Divine
"God work," 262
good versus evil, 199–200
Grof, Stanislav, 20
group interaction, dynamics of, 75

index

Hades, 106, 107, 111, 114
Hale-Bopp comet cult, 54
"hanging in the dangle," 233–35, 240
healthy diet, 212
heart, 195, 215
  authentic nature, 119
  coming from the, 221–23
  open, 119, 128
    as bridge to the Divine, 105,
      216–20
  wounded, 150–53, 221–23
heartwork, 219
Higher Power, 246
human being, as human and divine,
    60–61, 137–42, 203–5,
    259–60
human nature, as sinful, 138, 139

"I am," 155–62, 165
ideal self, 151
  imaging the, 145–46
ideals and idealization, 33, 49, 54,
    81, 82, 170, 179
identification. *See* attachment; "I am"
  and disidentification, 165–66, 246
idols. *See* ideals and idealization
imagery. *See* visualization
individuation, 36, 45, 50, 52, 59–62,
    127, 158, 203, 252
Infinity, 25
initiation, 122–23, 219–20, 241
inner voice/inner guide, 16
insight, 42. *See also* self-knowledge
instinct, 52, 54, 57
intellect, limitations of, 242

Jesus, 36, 139–40, 173, 193, 248
journal, spiritual, 66–67, 80, 82, 83,
    127
Joy, 121

giving birth to, 257–58
Jung, Carl G., 45, 52, 53, 93, 155,
    197, 198

Kitselman, A. L., 155–56
Koresh, David, 54

Last Supper, 139–40
loss. *See* mourning
love, 36–37, 119–21, 125, 129
  falling in, 22
  honoring the divinity of human,
    193–97
  ideal, 33
  learned by experiencing unlove, 15
  surrendering (in)to, 105, 125,
    224–25
  types of, 98, 121, 123, 124, 248
    divine, 128, 187, 217. *See also*
      desire nature
    erotic, 44
    mature/sacred, 44, 76, 121

Magdalene, 36
male–female dynamic, 120
marriage, 29–30, 33, 115
  extramarital affairs, 210–11. *See*
    also sexual compulsions
masculine- and feminine-style
  thinking, 58–59
masculine–feminine union, 31, 38,
    50, 76, 78, 100, 121, 124, 126
masculinity and femininity, 9, 22, 31
  balance of, 50, 60, 69, 72–74, 76–
    79, 88, 99, 169
  tension between, 199–200
materialistic view, 138–39
meditation, 81–82. *See also* nil point
merger. *See* union
Moses, 156

271

index

mother, archetypal devouring,
47–48
mourning, 42–44
mystical experience, 53–54
myths, 10, 27

near-death experiences (NDEs),
18–19
needs. *See* desire nature
nil point, 72, 199, 206–8

observer consciousness, 95, 96
Observer Self, 95, 104–5, 165
opposites. *See also* masculinity and
femininity; thinking
balance between, 73–74, 77, 100,
257, 258. *See also* shadow
work
joining/union of, 22, 119, 120, 126,
139, 202–3, 217, 258, 263
tension of, 9, 198–205, 217–18
order, in one's personal life, 62–66

Pan, 43–46
panic, 43
participation mystique, 52, 100
Persephone, 114–15, 241
power and powerlessness. *See*
empowered self; self-
empowerment
pregnancy, 89
presence, 190
projections, integrating one's, 170
Psyche
awareness of, 3
and Eros, story of, 2–3, 27–38
as feminine, 10
functions, 3, 4
nature of, 7–8, 11
roles, 124
writing on, 10

psyche, 2, 4
healthy, 2
seeking completion, 188–89
as soul, 4
unhealthy, 6
psyche's mirror, 2
psychospiritual guides, 134
psychospiritual integration, 6
psychospiritual learning, 136
psychospiritual truths, 134, 135, 186
psychotherapy. *See* rebirthing
Western, 259
puer/puer aeternus, 243–44

Ram Dass, 149–50
rebirthing, therapeutic, 17–18, 20,
227–29
recognition, as key to integration,
150
relationships, 169
death/ending of, 231–32
romantic, 169. *See also* marriage
secrets to spiritualize, 125
religion, 138
responsibility, 203. *See also*
victimhood

sacrifice, 111, 117–18, 250
as giving up versus taking on,
235–42
seed bearer, becoming a, 265–68
Seed Thoughts, 3, 12, 133–37
Self, 201
Divine, 50, 156, 182, 255
Higher, 206, 213, 248, 251, 254
human/Divine, 60–61, 209, 250
self. *See* "I am"
cultivating, 247–52
development of sense of, 250. *See
also* individuation
false, 28

index

as greater than its conditions,
146–50
highest, 151
that one was born to be
committing to, 213–15
imaging the, 145–46
self-empowerment, 251–52. *See also*
empowered self
accepting the mantle of, 252–54
self-knowledge, path of, 45, 90,
208–13, 250–51
self-sacrifice. *See* sacrifice
selflessness, from selfishness to
selfhood to, 250
sexual compulsions, 189–90. *See also*
marriage, extramarital affairs
sexual shadows, 171
sexual union, 126
sexuality, 44, 78
shadow, 6, 33, 70, 166–70, 198, 202
in Psyche myth, 34, 45
recognizing/discovering one's, 33–
34, 45, 71, 172–74, 200
repression and denial of one's, 81,
166–67, 170, 173
revealing one's, 171
sacred function, 170–73
shadow play, 175–76
shadow self, dialogue with, 175–76
shadow work, 34, 81, 169–73
shame, 189, 190
sleep, 116–18
soul, 4, 20, 251, 260. *See also* Divine
Self
longings of, 11
standing in the light of one's,
215–16
Soul, Spiritual, 8, 13, 15, 28
soul-based living, shift from ego-
dominated to, 235–36
soul-based psychology, 4–5

soul desire, 187
Soul Events, 8–9, 15, 26
soul journey, 16, 65, 134
soul maturity, path toward, 55
soul transformation, 227
Spirit, 2, 4, 8, 105, 124, 143, 203,
204, 209, 220, 255
spiritual bypass, 6
spiritual communities, 5
spiritual impulses, 53
spiritual journey, 41, 49
spiritual maturity, 108
spiritual practice, 6
spiritual psychology, 4, 5, 187, 259–
63, 265
Spiritual Soul, 8, 13, 15, 28
spiritual urges, splitting off from
human needs, 143
spirituality, false, 54
Star-Self, 255–56
subpersonalities, 158–60
suffering, 41, 49, 115, 178–79, 217,
218. *See also* distress
suicide, urge toward, 42, 43, 69, 107
surrender, 125, 236–39, 243–45. *See
also* love
symbols, 209–11. *See also* archetypes

thinking
masculine- and feminine-style,
58–59
using the powers of concrete and
abstract, 101–4
transcendence, 124
of one's conditions, 153–55
premature, 7, 76
yearning for, 11
transformation, 10, 12, 20–21, 38,
49, 51, 115, 122, 133, 226. *See
also* rebirthing
archetype of, 58

requirements for, 117
soul, 227
suffering and, 178–79
transformational journey, 134
Transformers: The Artists of Self-Creation (Small), 24, 25
"truth detector," 215
twelve-step groups, 160, 236–37

unconscious mind, as spectrum, 52
underworld, descending to the, 105–27, 226
union. *See also* opposites, joining/union of
loving, 23, 61, 124–26
through touch/sensation versus choice/will, 55
Upanishads, 144

vertical dimension, shifting from horizontal to, 246–47

victim consciousness, 176–78, 180–82, 184
victimhood, 176–82, 185
vision, inner, 136
visualization, 136

will, 76
withdrawal versus overinvolvement, 163–64
women. *See* masculinity and femininity
falling in love with an eternal youth, 243–44
fear of embodying masculine energy, 70
as relationship makers, 120
writing. *See* journal

yin and yang, 77. *See also* opposites
Yogananda, Paramahansa, 85

Zeus, 86–87, 89, 121

JACQUELYN SMALL is an internationally recognized workshop leader and author and pioneer in the emerging field of Spiritual Psychology. She is the author of eight books on personal transformation, including the classics, *Becoming Naturally Therapeutic*; *Transformers*; and *Awakening in Time*. She is the Founding Director of the Eupsychia Institute and certifies students in Psychospiritual Integration and Integrative Breathwork. She lives in Austin, Texas. For information on her work, see her website: EUPSYCHIA.com or call 1 800 546-2795.